HE

C000298101

HOOLIGAN

About the Author

Muthena Paul Alkazraji is a journalist, author and editor. His articles have been published broadly in the UK Christian press, including *Christianity Magazine* and *The Christian Herald,* and his travel articles have been published in *The Independent.* His first book *Love Changes Everything* is published by Scripture Union. His third book *Christ and the Kalashnikov* is published by Zondervan, and is set in Albania, where he currently lives and edits a magazine called 'Ujëvarë' for Albanian believers.

About Highland Books

Find out more at www.highlandbks.com

Heart of a Hooligan

Muthena Paul Alkazraji

Highland Books

GODALMING
SURREY

First published in 2000 by Highland Books,
Two High Pines, Knoll Road, Godalming,
Surrey GU7 2EP. Reprinted 2006, 2007

Cover design by Adrian Barclay

ISBN: 1 897913 52 4

Printed in Great Britain by CPI Bookmarque
Limited, Croydon.

CONTENTS

Author's Acknowledgements.

Thanks to Dave for letting me into your confidence. Thank you Val and Cliff. Thank you Mum and Colin for all your support.

Dave's Dedication.

To my mother, Dave and Tina, Nick and Babs and my special baby Hannah.

Chapter One

STOCKHOLM
SUBWAY

Tension amongst the England supporters in Stockholm's Rasunda Football Stadium was rising even higher. The match had been over for twenty minutes, and officials were showing no sign of allowing the thousands of fans out of the ground: they wanted to get the Swedish supporters well away. Directly behind the goalposts, a crowd of angry lads began rocking and dropkicking a plate-metal exit gate that was containing them in their defeat. They'd had just about enough.

It was June 17th 1992. Despite scoring a promising goal in the first half of their game against Sweden, England had conceded two in the second half, and were now decisively out of the European Soccer Championships. It was another depressing performance for the England fans. Earlier in the competition, disturbances had followed them across the country, and there had been scuffles before the Sweden game. The press had been trailing the fans on 'Hooli-watch', waiting and secretly hoping for the trouble to kick off, and it had been widely reported that the English 'hooligans' were coming to Stockholm. Rumours were circulating that 'The Black Army', a gang of Swedish lads were coming to confront the England fans, and security was now tight around the stadium. All along the approach roads, riot police clad in black uniforms and carrying Perspex shields were restraining guard dogs on their leads. Mounted officers were patrolling on horseback, and helicopters were hovering high above monitoring the movement of the crowds.

The England fans spilled out into the street as the stadium gates were pulled back. Dave Jeal, a six-foot Bristol Rovers supporter walked out confidently wearing a casual *Stone Island* jacket with the labels on its sleeves carefully ironed like some regimental insignia. He had caught a flight over from Gatwick especially for the match, and had hooked up with a crowd of Bristol City,

Leeds United and Crystal Palace men earlier in the day. At home they would all have been rivals, but on foreign soil these differences were put aside: together they were 'England'. Outside the gates a nine-foot high wire fence separated them from the yellow and blue stream of Swedish youths, and spittle and abuse was being freely exchanged through it. Suddenly, on the Swedish side, Dave noticed a group of England fans taking a beating, and they were totally out numbered. The adrenaline surged through him. He leapt onto the mesh, hooking his fingers through the wire squares, and then pulled himself higher until he could swing his leg over the top. He then sprawled over onto the concrete. The Bristol City boys followed on. Fifty metres along the fence, a swarm of England fans charged through a gap in the security. A chant rose up from the Swedish crowd, 'Black Army, Black Army, Black Army'. The two factions ran into each other and the fighting exploded.

One Swedish lad stood his ground dancing and kicking like a Thai boxer. Dave stormed past him and punched another lad hard in the head. The lad clasped his face and stumbled away. As quickly as it had erupted, the fighting thinned out and the 'Black Army' backed off. Dave turned around and saw a young man lying on the ground, hopelessly outnumbered by the England fans around him. Again and again he was being punched and kicked and putting up no resistance as the blows rained down on him. Dave flinched at the sight, but then ran on with the crowd chasing the Swedish youths as they scattered. A stocky man stepped out from behind a hot-dog van jeering and passing a baseball bat from hand to hand. A shower of bottles knocked him to the floor, and he too was kicked and punched. As Dave jogged back towards the mesh fence, he noticed the same fallen man he had seen ten minutes earlier. He was still surrounded by England supporters and the assault was continuing. Passers by were trying to pull the attackers off him. Again and again he was being viciously kicked. The man was lying slumped like a sack of rags. Blood was running from his body.

Dave turned and walked slowly away along the edge of the fence. He had never seen anything like this before. This was not how it was supposed to be. A few punches and a lot of front, yes, but this was something else. A feeling of nausea rose up from his stomach and he tried to swallow it down. His arms and legs were trembling. Tears began to smart at the back of his eyes and he wiped them away on his shirtsleeve. This was no longer an adventure: this was sheer evil. He lit up a cigarette and sucked hard on it. He blew out the smoke and drew deeply again.

Shortly, Dave met up with a couple of his mates. They had decided to go do some looting in the town centre, and they invited him to come along with them.

"I think I'll catch you later," he replied quietly. Then he slipped in amongst the crowds of other faces—some painted white with a red George cross over, others quietly downcast at England's defeat—until he was well away. Fifteen minutes later, he flagged down a dark, *Volvo* taxi and slid limply onto the rear seat. "You are English," the driver stated curiously. "What about all the trouble eh? Terrible…" Dave didn't reply. At the England supporter's campsite he thrust a couple of notes forward and then slammed the cab door firmly.

Later in the evening, Dave wandered around the tents in search of a call box. Through the compound fence he spotted a small, silver booth attached to a telegraph pole, and made his way around to it. He picked up the receiver, slotted in his phone card, and methodically pressed out the long digit sequence that he had written down on a small scrap of paper. He hoped that his mother would be at home. He felt desperate to talk to her. She was a member of the

Salvation Army, and though it had often been a right embarrassment to him, it might now be some small comfort.

"Mum? Mum…" he shouted anxiously, as if he were trying to reach back to England. "I'm really *scared*… Will you pray for me?"

"You've been in the trouble, haven't you?" she said softly. "I've seen it on the news."

"I feel alone mum," he said, his voice beginning to break. "Really alone…"

"It is okay Dave, you're not alone," she replied. A minute later, the spent card clicked out. Dave hung up the receiver and turned to look back along the empty street.

The Stockholm air felt heavy that night, as if some unseen presence were pressing itself down onto city with malice. Dave had found a place to sleep in the ground's changing rooms; he hadn't bothered to pack his tent this time. Inside the building it was dimly lit and silent, save for the drips of water falling from the showerheads and patting into small pools of water below. There was no one else here. The other boys were still out drinking or looting. Dave unfolded his sleeping bag and lay his head on his rolled up jacket. The hard tiled floor on which he was bedding down gave him little comfort. He tried to sleep but images of the violence outside the stadium, of the man slumped and bleeding, kept dancing at him in his mind's eye.

As he lay there in the early hours of the morning, he felt something begin to bare down on him – something tangible but unseen. It was as if it were trying to suffocate the life out of him, invade him and crush him, yet he could not see it or punch it off. The hairs on his arms were standing alert and his heart was thumping at his ribs. He flailed his limbs around but he could not dislodge it. He curled up in a ball, screwed his eyes tightly, and he heard himself whimper like some frightened animal.

The boys returned shortly after dawn. They had been out kicking up trouble in the city centre and were telling exaggerated stories of their escapades.

"Dave. Get out of the country mate!" said one lad looking down at him with a serious expression on his face. "They've got it all on video. It was just on their breakfast TV. They're looking for all the people fighting at the stadium. You know that Bristol City kid? Well he's been arrested…"

Dave felt a flash of deep fear. His plans to see the sights of Sweden were now nullified. He just wanted to get back home. He sat upright. He rolled up his sleeping bag and pulled on his *Adidas* trainers. He slung on his rucksack, and nodded at his mates. They looked across at him as they folded up their clothes hastily. It was five thirty in the morning. Dave let the changing room door bang behind him as he left.

Outside, the air was chilly and the sunlight sent long shadows from the tents stretching across the grass. Already people were milling around. At the fenced entrance to the campsite, the police were waiting. As the England supporters passed to and fro through a narrow gate, a group of Swedish officers were stopping everyone. Dave walked steadily forwards studying the situation as he drew closer. He could see that they were asking for passports. They were looking at the photographs and checking them against their clipboards. As he approached the entrance, he tried not to show any emotion. He reached into his rucksack pocket, drew out the little black book, and handed it over. The officer looked at Dave, scrutinising him carefully. He flicked through the pages glancing at the tiny image near the front. He then looked down at his grid of photos and back at Dave. Dave looked at the officer levelly. The officer glanced again at his photo-file. He stared at Dave again and handed it back. Dave took it between his fingers and walked forwards. He kept walking away from the gate. Outside the compound, the streets were almost empty. He began to jog along. The fresh morning air felt cold in his lungs.

Ten minutes later, Dave bounded down the steps into an underground station. He traced his finger along a map on the wall for the route to the city's Arlander Airport. Below him he could hear the faint screech of wheels on steel rails and the muffled rumble of the trains. There were very few people using the station at this hour of the morning, and there were no police here. He began to relax a little. He examined the unfamiliar coins in his wallet and slotted a few into the ticket dispenser. It spat out the square of card noisily onto its metal lip. Dave felt suddenly conspicuous. He looked around sharply. There was no one now in this section of the station. He took his ticket, walked across the stone floor, and fed it through the automatic barrier. Ahead of him the escalator trundled down steeply towards the train platforms. He stepped on to the top step and began to descend steadily. He watched the bare, posterless walls slide past, and glanced down at his watch. Thirty metres below him, a man in a black uniform stepped on to the upcoming escalator. Dave felt his heart beat faster. He looked back up the tunnel. There was no one above him. He could turn around and stride up the steps if he acted now. He looked back down the escalator. The man was staring directly at him. Dave looked away at the wall, and then furtively back at the man. He felt a cold sweat forming on his back: he could feel the man's eyes on him.

As the man drew closer he kept looking straight up at him. Dave noticed that his hat had a purple band around its rim. The uniform was not that of the Swedish police but of the Salvation Army. He couldn't believe it: here at 6am in a Stockholm subway! As he passed alongside, the man turned to him and smiled. His face was warm and peaceful. Dave watched him pass and then draw away. The man turned to look back down at him. Suddenly he felt the escalator level out beneath his feet, and he stumbled forward. He stared back up the steps. The man had gone. A feeling welled up inside him: *somehow now everything was going to be okay.*

Dave walked across the polished floor of the airport departures building half an hour later, and leant on the airline desk. His return flight was not for another two weeks but he was determined to fly home today. He asked the assistant to change his ticket.

"I'm afraid that isn't possible with your ticket type, sir," she replied.

"But you could do it for me, couldn't you?" he said, straining to smile with a little charm.

She repeated her response coolly. Dave slid a credit card out of his wallet and pushed it forward. The assistant glanced at her screen and tapped impassively at the keyboard. The next flight left in eight hours time. She keyed his details slowly into her computer, and then muttered something in Swedish to her colleague. Dave watched her as she moved her hands around below his view. Then she placed a folded cardboard envelope on the counter. He had his place on the plane.

The terminal building was swollen with thousands of other England supporters. Groups of downcast young men were killing time meandering around the cafes with their arms around each other's shoulders, waving their union jacks, and saluting each other in consolation with cans of lager. Others were lying on settees or sitting in huddles on the carpeted floor sections playing cards, chatting and singing. Swedish police officers were watching the fans discretely, patrolling through the building and stopping individuals from time to time to check their passports. Dave walked steadily over to a long stretch of windows and watched the baggage transporters snaking their way over the tarmac to the parked aircraft.

Away ahead of him a large British Airways jet was taxiing into position. It turned and stopped on the runway with its wing lights pulsing. Dave waited and watched. Suddenly, it accelerated across his field of view until its nose lifted up and it rose at a severe angle away into the low-hanging cloud base. Dave wished that he were on it. He turned around and made his way over to a burger outlet and bought a large coffee in a polystyrene cup. He placed it down on the counter, tipped in a sachet of sugar, and stirred it pensively with a thin plastic stick.

He had made his mind up that when he got back to England he was going to make a clean start. He was going to stay out of all the climbing over fences to look for trouble with rival fans that he'd got so wrapped up in. He was tired of all the aggro and the sleepless nights it had caused him. He felt sick about what he had seen outside the stadium. He felt sick of the whole scene.

A small group of lads were laughing and cracking English jokes nearby. Dave wandered over and sat alongside them on his rucksack. He chatted about England's poor performance and the price of flights out from the UK. Shortly, a couple of policemen walked over to the group. Dave began to breathe a little quicker.

"Can we see your passports please, boys," one officer asked in an authoritative tone. "Haven't you got any parking tickets to hand out?" quipped a big lad in a denim jacket.

Everyone smirked and began reaching into jacket pockets and unzipping holdalls. Dave held up his passport from the floor without looking directly at them. The officer thumbed officiously through the pages. He then looked back down at him, and back at his colleague. Dave tried his best to act naturally. He kept on talking to the person next to him, but inside he was pleading with something. He thought about the man on the escalator, and about his mother. He wanted to leave Stockholm behind him. He just wanted a chance to make a break.

Chapter Two

SOLDIER BOY

Dave lay silently on the floor of his grandparents' living room. His camouflaged army trousers and jacket blended into the dark green carpet making it difficult for any German patrol units to spot his position. His eye was fixed keenly on the sights of his toy machine gun. He could lie in wait, ready for an ambush, four hours and never tire of this game. "Where's Dave?" his granddad called out knowingly. "Has anyone seen Dave?" Dave rolled out from behind the settee, sprang to his feet, legs astride, and let out a burst of automatic fire. "Rat-tat-tat-tat-tat," he shouted.

"Stand to attention," barked his grandfather. "Quick... *march*. Left-right-left. Left-right-left. Halt. Wait for it, lad. About...

turn." Dave proudly obeyed his granddad's orders, marching backwards and forwards, swinging his stiff little arms high above his shoulders in time to the drill commands. When he grew up, he was going to be a soldier.

During the Second World War, Dave's granddad, 'pops', had been a Sergeant Major in the King's Liverpool Irish Regiment, and he was the little boy's hero. Dave would sit on his knee and ask him to bring out his treasured photograph album, his buffed medals, his hat and cane. He would balance the oversized hat on his head and ask for another of his incredible war stories. One time in France, after stealthily crossing a minefield, he and the borstal boys he had made into soldiers captured a farm house full of German officers, drunk their *schnapps* and helped themselves to the humiliated men's personal effects. On another occasion, whilst serving with a regiment in India, he had drunk a round or three of beer, climbed up the Taj Mahal, and cried out a loud call to prayer. Later, he had been severely disciplined for this escapade. Dave was all ears; he could not hear enough.

Dave knew, though, that his granddad wasn't well. Sometimes 'pops' seemed silent and distant, as if his sparkle had ebbed away. If anyone made a sudden noise in the house, he would tense his shoulders and grip the arm of his chair. He had taken part in the D-Day landings, and later, following a battle at Nijmegen in Holland, had been sent to a mental hospital in Scotland. For two years Dave's Nan had not been allowed to visit him, and later she could only do so with a soldier present. Whatever he had witnessed in the Allied push across The Netherlands had left him emotionally damaged and shell-shocked. It seemed to Dave from his granddad's war stories that the Japanese were a cruel and evil people, that the French were not tough enough as a nation to see off the Nazi's themselves, and that if the Dutch had fought their own battles, his granddad would not now be ill.

Sometimes as a Saturday night treat, Dave's Nan and granddad would let him remain up later than his usual 8pm bedtime. He loved every minute of staying at their house. His Nan would bring him a plate of cheese and biscuits and a mug of milky coffee, and he would settle into the warmth between them on his own special cushion. There in the half-light of the television screen he'd wait for the highlight of the evening's viewing: 'Match of the Day'. Dave loved the excitement in the crowd before the game began, the tension as the attack and counter-attack swung play backwards and forwards into each team's half of the pitch, and the surge of noise that erupted when one team scored. It was here that he watched Leeds United Versus Bayern Munich in the 1975 European Cup Final, cheering Leeds along to win, even though they lost.

Dave's mum, Val, had left his father in 1967 when he was one year old to live back with her parents in Stoke Gifford, a bungalowed suburb of the city. Her marriage was making her deeply unhappy and she was suffering from depression as a result. Dave was a hyperactive child and was on medication to sedate him. As early as his memory serves him he was in some kind of trouble, and felt constantly worried about the consequences of something that he'd done that might well soon be discovered. Not untypically, he had a pet tortoise called Tommy (a female it later transpired) and he was told not to wake it up during its hibernation period. Dave wanted to do things his way: he wanted to play now. He woke it, and Tommy died. For days he felt sheepish and uneasy about it. On another occasion, after he had mouthed off his mum, he remembers her grabbing him by his jumper in frustration and washing out his mouth with foul carbolic soap. If Dave wasn't hammering nails through his bedroom carpet, he was snapping his possessions into pieces.

Val met and married a quiet photographic technician, Cliff, when Dave was five years old, and they left her parents' home to live on a modern housing estate in Yate on the edge of the city. Not long after, Cliff built him a large toy fort and tank from a plastic assembly kit. Dave raised his fists and smashed them to bits. He didn't want them. He just wanted to be alone with his mum, and he thought that Cliff might take her away. Cliff tried hard to love him as a dad, but as Dave grew a little older they clashed frequently. Dave was still continuously hyperactive and always in trouble, and it fell to Cliff to administer the punishment. When he did so, Dave felt that his mother was being treacherous for not taking his side.

When Dave was left with child-minders, they too would have to tackle his difficult behaviour—sometimes in ways that left their marks. On one occasion, he was made to sit on a hard wooden stool without moving for hours until his mum came home. Eventually, as on many other days in Yate, he ran away to the bottom of the garden. Here, he got down on his hands and knees, and scrambled over the leaves and cracking twigs into the undergrowth. Between two branches, where the bark was worn and smooth, he hooked his leg through and the bush swayed as it took his weight. On all sides he was concealed by a veil of leaves. Now, no one could see him here. He was tired of always being in trouble. Often, he would sit here for hours, tears patting onto the backs of his hands and running down along the folds in his trousers.

The family moved across the city to live close to the council estates of Southmead when Dave was eight years old. Here, Dave and his best mate William, a curly-haired boy with a turned-up nose, got into further trouble together. Some of it was boyish mischief, but some of it gave others more serious cause for concern. Together, he and William hid in the swaying summer grass on the edge of Filton Golf Course. When a golf ball landed close by, Dave would scuttle out and swiftly bring it back to their stash in the rough. The afternoons passed as they filled their carrier bags until the polythene handles broke. Later, they would sneak along to the clubhouse shop and sell them all back again. It kept them both nicely in extra pocket money.

One time, after a local building contractor heaped mounds of black mud on a nearby site, Dave and William discovered a large collection of human bones that had come from an unearthed burial ground. They gathered up a large sack full of sculls, took them home and washed them, and then began trying to hawk them around the neighbourhood on offer at 50p a piece. When the police got wind of it, they were none too happy.

More seriously, on another occasion, Dave loosened the taps on the back of an Esso petrol tanker sending a current of fluid gushing along the road. When the driver arrived, he and another friend scarpered. Dave waited anxiously for days expecting the police to arrive. He escaped this offence without punishment, but he was, however, caught for a further misdemeanour when the police paid a visit to search his bedroom. Cliff had rightly suspected that he was concealing a small store of live rifle cartridges there. The men ticked him off, but with some discomfort. Dave had gathered them up from the nearby police firing range where they had been left discarded on the ground. He had kept them hidden for some time below a false bottom he had set up in his laminated Formica wardrobe. It was here also that he kept his 'secret box', a small container which held a knife, a box of matches, a magnifying glass, a bag of peanuts and other survival items. It was ready there for if he ever had to escape or run away. One day, he thought, there might well be a war.

From his earliest days at school, Dave was restless and in trouble. At nursery, other parents complained to the staff that he had hit their children, and his mother was called in and informed of his behaviour. At his first primary school, he got into more fights, pulling the buttons off a boy's shirt, and on one occasion he lunged at another child with a pencil, marking him on the face. That day, Dave stood outside the classroom door in the empty morning corridor knowing this time he was in deeper trouble. Later, his mother came to take him home: she had been asked to remove him permanently. At his next primary school in Yate, he performed poorly in most subjects, a trend that was to continue throughout the remainder of his school days.

He did not want to do badly in class, he often tried his hardest, but he could not seem to arrange letters and numbers so easily, or even remember instructions, and this seemed to trip him up. He was told repeatedly that he was lazy, stupid and disruptive. When he was referred to an educational psychologist, his difficulties were attributed not to a lack of intelligence, but to having come from a broken home.

At a further primary school in Southmead, his class teacher would knock him hard on the head with a board rubber.

"Con-Jeal," he'd repeat on an almost daily basis, "You're a bit of a clot. You're a bit of a clot."

Dave just wanted more time to do things, and a little more help, but often he had to work on his own doing separate activities from his peers. Because of this, he desperately wanted to show that he was good at something, and one strength he did have was a wide general knowledge. He could remember the details of historical events and the names and locations of countries, cities and rivers with ease. When quizzes were held in class, his arm shot up like the door on a greyhound trap to almost every question, and regularly he was right.

But this too irritated his teacher. "Put your hand down Jeal," he'd say wearily. Dave consequently turned his feelings inward. A small compensation for his self-esteem, however, came outside in the playground—and often in class when the teacher's back was turned. Every week he would bring along a couple of his chipped and scuffed marbles. With these he would harvest a bag-full of clear glass, rainbow–spiral and ocean-blue jewels. Dave took on all-comers and stripped them of their pocket treasures, to the point that no one would give him a game. Around a circle of chalk on the pavement, Dave deserved two gold stars, but no one ever gave them out.

One teacher alone stands out as someone who would warmly receive him throughout his early days at school. Mr Maxwell was an ageing former RAF pilot with a classic handlebar moustache. He had fought the Japanese in the Pacific in the Second World War, and flown on combat missions in a Spitfire aircraft. Dave would seek him out at dinnertime, hungry for his fantastic aerial dogfight stories. During a sortie, Mr Maxwell had swooped down so low over a Japanese trench that he had taken off the heads of two soldiers with the blade of his wings. Dave was wide-eyed with wonder. Other times, when Dave brought in stones, fossils and owl pellets from his rummaging expeditions to the local dump, Mr Maxwell would help him attach them to little pieces of mounting board before analysing and labelling them in detail. Dave found the process fascinating.

For a single Sunday every month, Dave was obliged to see his real father. He never felt wanted or valued by him during these visits. One afternoon, in the back garden of his self-built, five-bedroom house, Dave's dad, a former professional footballer, challenged him to a little game for his pocket money.

"If you can put three past me Dave, I'll double it," he announced.

Dave picked up the football and positioned it exactly twelve paces from his father. His father crouched ahead of him between two jackets set down on the grass for goal posts. Dave ran up and booted the ball hard to his right, and it slipped past the tips of his dad's outstretched fingers. Dave could feel the excitement welling up inside him. Next, he slipped a second shot tidily through his father's legs.

"It's double or quits Dave," said his father. Dave began to feel a little uncertain. He put the ball back on the penalty spot, took three steps back, and kicked it. With little effort his dad trapped it dead under his foot. "Sorry Dave," he said. "I win."

Dave hung his head and kicked the grass. He knew that he'd been tricked. This game was played out again and again, and Dave kept running right into it.

Dave got back in his own way. He annoyed his father, irritated him or stole things, be that a few coins lying around on the kitchen table or silver change from one of his stepsisters' swollen piggy banks. It seemed to him that his father's family had so much, and little of that came his way. He simply wanted his father to want him.

On another Sunday visit, he was taken to a party in the next door neighbour's garden. It was a sunny summer's afternoon and the adults who mingled and chatted, serving themselves to food from the extensive buffet table seemed not to notice him. Neither did his father. Dave wandered around the tables and chairs accidentally knocking over a plate of food. A man in an expensive suit spun around and swore at him. He had never heard an adult say such a thing before and he felt shaky. He drifted around further and saw his father laughing with a crowd of people he did not know.

On the top of an empty table he noticed a shiny, black JPS container packed tightly with complementary cigarettes for the guests. He looked around him. He snatched a handful and slotted them into his inside jacket pocket. On another empty table he helped himself to more. For a further fifteen minutes he roamed around, surreptitiously filling up his pockets, and no one saw him. He grabbed an open can of *Heineken*, tucked it up his sleeve, and made his way to the toilet. He slid the latch to lock the door. No one came or knocked. His father did not come to find him. Dave sat on the toilet seat and savoured the lager. He felt a warm glow of resentful satisfaction.

Chapter Three

KNOCKS ON THE PLAYING FIELD

"**O**i, you kid," came a voice from further back on the school bus. "I'm talking to you…" The hum of voices quietened down. "You think you're special, don't you? You posh snob."

There was a snickering now. Dave felt something wet land on the back of his head. He passed his hand slowly over his hair and looked at his fingers. Spittle was dribbling over them. He wanted to look around but he knew it would make things worse. He sat motionless, hoping that nothing else would happen. He felt the beads of cold perspiration gather on his forehead, and his stomach begin to twist. Right now he would have given anything to be back at home in the quiet safety of his bedroom.

The bus driver was just a few yards away, his hands feeding the wheel from right to left with a firm confidence. He felt a little safer. It wasn't far now to the school. Something else landed on his black blazer sleeve. Other pupils were giggling now. Dave hated wearing his school uniform: no one else bothered with them. His mother had bought him it and she was now insisting. He looked down at the polished briefcase at his feet. He had tried to scuff and wipe some dirt on it, but it shone like a new pair of silly shoes.

Three youths stumbled down the aisle as the bus drew up alongside the school fence, and stood swaying around on the handrail above him. Dave looked up at them nervously. "Alright?" he said. They did not reply.

The boys were wearing Dr Marten's boots and Crombie coats, and two of them had thin tramlines cut through the close-cropped hair above their ears. As the bus braked, one youth swung round on the rail and smacked Dave's cheek with his fist. His head bounced off the window as it rolled sideways. A sharp pain bit at both sides of his mind. Dave pressed into the soreness with his hands to ease it.

The youths jumped of laughing. The driver saw nothing. Other pupils jostled boisterously past him. Dave felt sick and it was just 8.45 am. It was becoming a regular thing, and he knew it would happen again. Dave wiped the spittle from his blazer with his hand, and smeared it under the seat.

From the age of eleven, Dave caught two buses every day to get from his home in Southmead to Lawrence Weston School four long miles away. He attended the school for five years, and he dreaded every single morning. He was also a small and skinny child. At Lawrence Weston the kids were tough, and the bullying and taunting came his way thick and fast. His old friends were at other schools now, and from the outset he felt he was different from the other pupils there. Even when his mother let him choose his own clothes at a later date, they were never quite the 'in' selection at Lawrence Weston.

At home Dave's parents had played him classical music, and though he liked chart and rock music, when he was able to identify pieces of Saint-Saens and Wagner in music lessons, it marked him out for further ridicule.

Dave tried to deal with the threat of bullying from other kids by mucking about, playing the joker and being cheeky. He figured that if he could make them laugh, then he might escape a fisting. Though this helped get those off his back who threatened to do him serious physical damage, it landed him in trouble with the teachers. Dave ended up in the midst of incidents on a regular basis, sometimes with a guilty face but often as a scapegoat for others.

His low popularity with the teaching staff was in no way further helped by his academic performance, which continued to be poor. A reputation for being a pest meant that he got less attention, and when he couldn't do the work he became a disruptive influence on others. All these things ensured that Dave was on 'daily report' for his full five years at the school. At the end of every lesson, he would have to present himself to the teacher, and take their comments home on a slip of paper for his parents to monitor.

It seemed to Dave sometimes that even some of the teachers were out to get him. One time on the playing fields, the rugby master instructed him to stand three yards ahead of the other pupils.

"Now lads, this is how you do a tackle," he grinned. He then ran at Dave, grasping his legs with his full body weight, and felled him flat in the cold mud. The force left Dave's ribs and shoulders aching, and his PE kit was wet and caked in dirt. "Get up lad," he ordered, and walked back to join the other boys.

The demonstration followed again. "Get up, lad," he repeated. Dave slithered back to his feet. "Now lads, this is how you do a hand off," he announced with a swaggering authority.

Again he ran at Dave, spread his hand over his face and squashing his nose he slammed him back down to the ground. Dave felt the size of a rugby ball. He knew this was more than a training display. This teacher was not the only one to single him out for their own brand of antagonism.

On another occasion at Lawrence Weston, the atmosphere in the school erupted into a riot amongst a group of pupils. Fire extinguishers were let off, walls were scrawled with black marker pens, and two doors were wrenched off their hinges and tossed through the windows of the English block. They crashed amidst a shower of glass onto the headmistress' car. Dave was summoned to the deputy-head's office. It was assumed that if he were not a principal culprit, then he would know who they were.

The man, an ex-Royal Marine with a thick beard, leaned across his desk and addressed him in an authoritative tone. "If you don't tell me who is responsible, I'll call your mother and get her down here."

Dave knew that if she came and believed him, he would likely get a caning from his stepfather. He had taken no part in the events, but he had seen them. The deputy-head waited, fixing his gaze on Dave. The room was quiet except for the click of lock mechanisms as doors closed in a nearby corridor. There was shouting outside in the playground. Dave sat on a plastic chair looking down at his shoes, and thought about what he should do. He knew that whatever he said he would be in trouble with someone. He thought about his grandfather, and about him fighting the Nazi's at Nijmegen. He imagined him held captive by the SS in some Bavarian castle, being inter- rogated and threatened with 'consequences' if he didn't reveal certain information. He thought about what 'pops' would do, and he knew what he was going to do. He kept looking at his shoes and said nothing.

When his mother arrived, she did not believe that he had been involved, and she told the deputy-head so. Dave felt her put her hand on his shoulder and they left the room together.

Later, some of those who had led the trouble cornered him; they knew that he'd been to the office. "If you've grassed Jeal," said one lad raising his fist, "then you'll get some more of this."

Dave felt no loyalty to them, and he did not account for himself, he just nodded.

At home, Dave's parents struggled to help and discipline him. Here too he continued to get into regular trouble, and he was generally unsettled and unhappy. One Spring term, he went with the school on a two-week trip to Ebermannstadt in Bavaria. On the way home, as he sat on the coach's back seat, he accidentally dislodged an ashtray, and someone told the driver that he had wrecked it.

The man protested bitterly to Val and Cliff when they arrived to collect him. "He's a bloody hooligan," he shouted. "That lad has smashed up my coach!"

Cliff was furious. Back at Southmead, he ordered him to get upstairs and wait. Fifteen minutes later, Dave stood balanced on the edge of the bath craning his neck towards the cabinet mirror to look at his backside. It was covered in a grid of red stripes, and they hurt like hell. Though a caning was exceptional, Dave got smacked at home regularly. Sometimes he reaped what he had sown, on other occasions he took an unfair punishment. It was hard for anyone to know if he had or hadn't been up to no good.

To help Dave with his schoolwork, Val arranged some extra maths tuition. One evening in the kitchen, she and Cliff tried to help him with the eight-times-table.

Their frustration began to build as they chanted it to him again and again. "What is seven times eight Dave?"

Dave blurted out anything that came into his head. "Forty eight..." He just couldn't get his head around numbers, nor could he remember birthdays or telephone numbers for that matter.

"You're being stupid Dave. Listen... Seven times eight is fifty-six. What is seven times eight?"

"I don't know. I don't know," he screamed.

His mother snapped. She reached for a large pot of yoghurt on the table and smashed it down on his head. Dave sat there shaking, the white fluid dribbling over his cheeks and shirt. He just couldn't do it, and he fought back the tears.

The warmth of his Nan and granddad's house was now on the other side of the city, and Dave began to clasp around for sources of comfort and escape. From all sides in his mind he could hear the voices of people telling him that he was a waster, trouble and bad news. Like many kids he had started smoking, and he used his dinner money to buy cigarettes before trading them in the playground for more money.

Sometimes he managed to buy a bottle of cider and swig it secretly with a friend. On other days, he would find a secluded place outside, pour some *Tippex* thinners or *Evostick* into a plastic bag, and hold it over his mouth, drawing in steady lung-fulls of the vapour. Soon a creeping numbness would enfold him. It was an exit of a kind for a few hours.

When Dave left Lawrence Weston School at the age of fifteen, he had three high grade CSE's, and six low. He found a job at a Bristol engineering company that made prison doors and windows. Here he began to learn how to use an angle grinder and how to cut and shape metal, but as the youngest lad in the firm he quickly became the butt of customary shop floor apprentice-baiting.

The older men cornered him near the sawing machines, pinned him to the floor, removed his overalls and rubbed Swarfega down his pants. On another occasion they sprayed him with red oxide. One of Dave's jobs was to make the tea for everyone, and when they weren't happy with the brew they would sling it at him. At first he could see it was a bit of a laugh, but when it persisted the joke wore thin. He'd had his fill of hassle, and left after a couple of months fed up and bored with the work.

He secured himself a job shortly at a small business specialising in screen and litho printing. His role was to be the general dogsbody: to do this and that as others in the shop required. The work was tedious and physical: counting and collating the printed sheets, and cleaning carefully around the machines.

One day, a secretary asked Dave to wipe the ink from some silk screens gesturing towards a bottle of thinners and a cloth. There was just something about the manner in which she said it. It was as if her words were the little jab that edged him over a line: he was now so hair-trigger sensitive. Dave felt that he had had enough of her and this place and everyone. He spun around and spat out a stream of abuse at her telling her what she could do with her screens. If anybody else had a go at him now they too were going to get what they had coming to them.

The secretary reported the incident to the manager. Dave was shortly asked to leave. From then on, the pattern for his working life was set. Dave moved from job to job getting sacked because of his attitude.

For a short period of time, Dave enrolled at Bristol's Brunel Technical College on a course in engineering and computing. The government was giving an additional benefit payment to those who attended the new scheme, and he thought that he'd take up their offer. Dave didn't really understand the lectures, and he and many others on it had little real motivation for the subject. As a consequence, the situation in class soon degenerated. Fights broke out; they broke into machines in the college refectory, and flooded the floor of a classroom by holding paper boat races in a specialist wave machine.

Whilst roaming the corridors of the catering department, they discovered a modest Christmas feast laid out in preparation for the arrival of a number of civic dignitaries, including the mayor. The centre-piece was a huge, bronzed roast turkey. The boys ripped off its legs and stripped the carcass of meat leaving little more than a pile of bones, and then helped themselves to the rest of the spread. It was soon discovered, and they were all presently expelled.

Dave soon found himself a new crowd along the city's busy Gloucester Road. From the streets of the adjacent districts of Lockleaze and Horfield the local lads, Bristol Rovers supporters, would gather to drink and play pool at the Royal Oak and Sportsman pubs, or to crawl the drinking spots along the main road's length. It was the year of Britain's victory in the Falklands conflict, and Dave and his mates revelled in nationalistic pride by dialling random telephone numbers in Argentina and shouting abuse into the receiver.

Gangs from rival areas of the city would roll in on a Saturday night, and, as the locals banded together to taunt and see them off, fights would break out on a regular basis. Sometimes after such evenings, Dave would leave his clothes to soak overnight in his mother's bath. On Sunday mornings the cold water would be pink with the blood – his own and other people's.

A taste for the thrill of street combat saw Dave arrested and appearing in court for the first in a number of incidents when one exchange resulted in the smashing up of a taxicab. He was seventeen, and his ideas of joining the army were dashed. He was devastated about it: it was the death of a childhood ambition. A diverting pursuit, however, was firmly taking a hold of him.

One warm summer's evening, a group of Gloucester Road lads hired a coach to transport them on a stag night to the nearby Georgian city of Bath. The gang toured the pubs as the hours passed, filling themselves with beer and scuffling with each other and anyone else who gave them a glance of disdain. As closing time approached, a fight broke out when a doorman refused them entry. The police were called and they were escorted back to their coach. As they drove out of the city the mayhem erupted. The emergency door was pushed open in the path of an oncoming lamppost. It rammed into the metal spraying shards of glass across the interior as it ricocheted back.

Over the twelve miles home many of the remaining windows were put through, the seats were ripped up and the interior trashed. As the driver steered the shell of his vehicle towards a police station with the culprits still on board, one by one they jumped out as the coach slowed down at intersections. As it drove along Bristol's Muller Road, Dave decided he would make a leap for it. He hung his legs out of a passenger window, nicking his palms on the glass fragments in the frames as the cool wind blew past, and launched himself out onto the black tarmac. He hit the road surface with a smack and began to tumble over and over. To his left he saw the wheel of the coach. He seemed to roll in closer. Its silver hubcap was spinning. Then he blacked out.

When he awoke, he was lying at the side of the road. His shirt was ripped and marked with large dark scuffs. He had cuts and bruises on his shoulders and face, but he was otherwise unharmed. He looked back at the road and thought about the coach wheel. He was amazed and shaken. It seemed to him that he was alive by some preserving intervention.

Chapter Four

THE BLUE KICKERS

Bristol Rovers Football Club were playing Gillingham away, and Dave had driven along the motorway in a hired transit van to watch the match with a crowd of mates from the Gloucester Road scene. The group had decided to stand amongst the Gillingham supporters as a show of bravado, and in between watching play on the pitch they taunted a crowd of nearby lads. Dave and his mates had taken to wearing designer label clothing – *Burberry* and *Christian Dior* or *Fila* and *Taschini* tracksuits—without their club's blue and white colours. On the terraces it made a clear and recognised statement: if you want some trouble, then we're up for it.

Dave singled out a stocky youth who had flicked his hair self-consciously to one side. "What sort of shoes do you call those then? They used to be 'in', didn't they? When was it? Last year some time?" he mocked.

The lad looked down at his blue *Kickers*. The Bristol boys fell about laughing. They were now wearing *Clarks'* desert boots with *Kickers* tags sewn on and felt roundly superior. The taunting and face off continued until the police picked out the Bristol boys and marched them back to their own end. "We'll see you later," a Gillingham supporter called after them.

"Oh yes! When you're ready," shouted Dave.

As Dave queued up with his mates for a serving of fish and chips near the ground, half an hour after the final whistle, a solitary Gillingham supporter strolled past the wide glass window and stepped up into the shop. He leant confidently on the buffed metal counter and looked across at them.

"Rovers were pretty useless today weren't they?" he grinned, glancing outside the door.

Dave couldn't believe it; this idiot was totally outnumbered. One of the group grabbed his freshly served Cornish pasty and rubbed it hard in the lad's face. As he staggered backwards, the door burst open and a gang of lads tumbled in brandishing Jif lemon squeezers like toy pistols.

A jet of clear fluid splattered across Dave's face. It smelt like bleach. His eyes began to sting viciously, and he doubled up trying to wipe them clean with his sleeve. Then a blow fell on his head and a foot rammed up across his nose and mouth. He flailed out wildly striking the air. Then he tumbled forwards across a bench and slumped to the floor trying to block further blows with his forearms.

He could smell the fat on the tiles and hear screaming. He tried to squint through the gap in his arms to get a look at his attacker. Through the water in his eyes he could see little but outline shapes. Another foot slammed into his chin. This time he saw what he needed to: the lad was wearing a pair of blue *Kickers*.

From the age of seventeen, Dave began to attend Bristol Rovers matches regularly both at home and away. Every Saturday, along with a crowd of other lads, he began to seek out that contingent in a rival club's supporters who were looking for the same kind of action. Such groups are known as 'firms' and their members 'boys' or 'casuals'. Dave felt a new kind of bond to his fellow 'boys', and his inclusion made him feel like he was someone special.

The occasional kicking from a rival was of little or no deterrence; a few battle wounds carried a certain kudos. The danger came with the thrill, and such events as those in Gillingham were the occupational hazard. It was all a wild source of adventure. On one occasion in Wales, where trouble flared up regularly with both Bristol clubs, a fellow Rovers 'boy' mistook Dave for a Bristol City supporter, and smashed out one of his teeth. When anyone else put one over on Dave and his mates, however, they would always try to find a way of getting even. One tactic was to arrive early on a match day, find out where the rival 'casuals' had parked their cars, and lie in wait for them after the game. If they couldn't return a kicking, 'a shoeing', they would smash up the vehicle for good measure. The Gillingham 'boys' eventually received such a treatment.

At home matches, a zeal for invading the pitch, climbing over fences to get into the away end, and shouting abusive language at rival supporters, saw Dave officially banned from the Rovers ground on two occasions. He managed to get both of them revoked, however, after pleading telephone calls to club officials. More importantly for Dave, though, such antics won him credibility on the terraces.

One time, Millwall FC came to play Rovers at the Eastville Stadium in Bristol. When the match was well underway, Millwall built up a mound of wood pieces on the stands and set it ablaze. As the smoke and flames belched out, they began to dance around the flames chanting, 'The lion is out of the den…The lion is out of the den,' like a tribe performing some unholy rite. They continued the taunting by hanging over the fence of the north enclosure waving fists full of notes and shouting, 'Loadsamoney. We've got Loadsamonaaay,' and 'Ooo aaar, ooo aaar' at the West Country lads.

A hail of copper coins flew from the Rovers fans showering the heads of the Londoners. Millwall launched their own rain of coinage back. Dave singled out a likely victim and crept out of eyes' view along the edge of the stand. He then squatted directly below the Millwall fan, who was leaning over the fence parading the contents of his wallet. Dave leapt up and snatched away a twenty-pound note. He then walked forwards and held it aloft to the home fans like a trophy. A large cheer went up. He felt brilliant.

"Oh, come on mate. Give us it back," the guy pleaded. Dave was having none of it.

At away matches, Dave and other 'boys' would try to take as many liberties as they could by swanning around town centres as if they owned the place, and cheeking off the locals. Away teams arriving in Bristol would do the same: it was the throwing down of a gauntlet.

Often they would try to find the pubs where the local 'boys' drank, and the locals would seek out the places where the incoming 'boys' were gathering to drink too. One drizzling autumn Saturday, Dave travelled up to Luton for an FA Cup tie. The city's team, Luton Town, were known to have a large 'firm' who called themselves The MIGS—an acronym for 'Men in Gear' on account of the fashion for designer clothing.

Dave was in a firm called 'The Young Executives'. Today they wore their smart blazers with the Bristol coat of arms on the chest pocket, and Dave had taken to wearing a nine-carat gold ring through each ear. Rovers had taken up coach loads of supporters, and many of them had been drinking along a street of pubs in the city centre. Dave knew that there would be trouble and he was pumped for it. Early afternoon the cry went up that the MIGS had come for them.

The Rovers fans snatched pool cues and balls as weaponry and ran outside. A large group of lads were walking slowly down the middle of the street. As the gangs ran at each other, a big youth wearing a smart leather jacket began to jog towards Dave beckoning with his hands.

"Come on then. Let's have it," he sneered.

Dave waited until he was closer. He took out a black pool ball, rolled it slowly in his fingers, and launched it at him. It struck him on the forehead and he jolted to a stop, his eyes bewildered. Dave watched as if events were now happening in slow motion. A huge lump swelled up above his eyebrows like an extra nose. Dave thought that he looked like a Darlek. The youth fell over backwards. Dave kicked him for good measure, and then ran on chasing the other MIGS.

The skirmishes continued outside the ground. The two groups of supporters charged and retreated from each other throwing graceless, ugly punches. A Luton youth stepped forward bullishly and stood his ground. One of Dave's mates, a short, muscular lad, ran forward, jumped up and butted him on the nose as if he were heading a corner ball down into the net. The youth dropped to his knees clasping his face, and the Luton fans backed off like warriors with a beaten leader. Rovers laughed at them, flicking their hands up and down in a gesture of contempt.

Shortly, one of the MIGS shouted to a policeman that Dave was carrying a knife.

The officer strode over and began to frisk him. The accusation was a lie, but he was going to check it out thoroughly. He ordered Dave to drop his trousers. Dave couldn't believe it. He looked around. His mates were sniggering. The policeman felt slowly along his jacket and trouser lining. He took out his wallet, and then, with the search complete, tossed it into a puddle of water.

"Clear off boy before I nick you," he barked. Dave sneered back at him.

As Dave approached the entrance to the stands, the two rival groups of supporters were passing through adjacent turnstiles separated only by a wire mesh fence. Both sides were spitting relentlessly at each other. One lad, defiant in the face of the coating he was taking, stood close in to the fence. His head and clothing were glistening with saliva, and he was spitting back like some feral creature.

"Yeah. Yeah. Come on then," he taunted, opening his mouth to shout abuse.

Dave stopped to watch. In an instant his mate began to snort and clear his lungs of phlegm. Then, thrusting his head forward, he spat the substance through the fence, and it flew straight into the Luton fan's mouth. The lad began to cough and wretch. All who saw it winced with laughter.

On the terraces, the resentment soon built up amongst the Rovers fans as Luton began to inflict a runaway defeat on the pitch. Each time the home team scored, a tiny dancing man would jig its way across an electronic scoreboard above the blue and white supporters. It seemed to taunt them in their humiliation. A piece of concrete was launched up at it, and then another one over the fence at the crowds of nearby Luton fans. The chunk came sailing back, and Dave stumbled away as it bounced along the ground and shattered into pieces.

Ahead of him, seat bottoms were now being torn up and hurled around like lethal Frisbees. Dave yanked at a metal railing loosening concrete pieces at its base, and then added his missiles to the growing exchange. Soon the police came swarming into the stands. Their dogs were set loose and bounded up the steps snarling with vicious intent. The crowds surged in different directions banging into each other to escape.

Dave was still shaking with the thrill of it all half an hour later. His blood was coursing through him, and he felt dizzy and alive. He looked around for his mates. He wanted to know if they were okay. One friend, a beanpole of a lad, walked stiffly across with a torn leather jacket and raw dog teeth marks in his side. Dave inspected the cuts. Others arrived and they were all largely fine. They joked and shoved each other around a bit. Dave looked back up at the scoreboard. It had taken a severe pounding from a hail of debris; all that was left of the dancing man was a single waving arm.

The code of behaviour amongst many 'casuals' was not one of merciless cruelty to their rivals in fights. When a lad had taken sufficient punishment, others would often jump in to stop it. Though Dave could deal out a beating, a 'slap', to those who were looking for it, he was not beyond protecting someone when the odds were well against them. One time, he noticed a West Bromwich Albion 'boy' standing alone in the Rovers end of the ground, perhaps for want of a ticket in the away section. His clothes were the give-away: Dave knew all the Rovers 'casuals'.

He stepped up quietly behind him. "Alright mate!" he said.

The lad looked around nervously. He knew he'd been spotted and that he could now get a serious kicking. Dave stood alongside him. "Just keep quiet, stay with me, and you'll be all right," he said.

"Cheers," the lad replied. They talked about each other's 'firms', and when the game was over, Dave saw him off the terraces without incident.

Many clubs had their own contingent of National Front supporters. Often, they would mark the party's logo and club name across Union Jacks and then proudly display them at matches. As some of Dave's mates adopted fascist thinking, he too drifted along with it, joining in with the salutes and chants of *'Zeig Heil'*, and the taunting of black players down on the pitch. The thought of his grandfather fighting against the Nazi's, however, made him feel very ill at ease with himself.

On one occasion he went along to a National Front meeting in the skittle alley of a local pub. He was surprised by the cross section of people present: academics and professionals as well as the expected angry-looking skinheads. What had been posturing on the terraces now struck him as a disturbing business in reality as the actual proceedings got underway. When an Indian politics student present was verbally abused, Dave and a friend tried to apologise to her outside. He felt ashamed. She, though, was doubly scathing of them; not only were they racists, but they did not even have the courage of their own convictions. Dave did not attend again, and after this he kept his views silent. For many 'boys' on the terraces, if you were not a 'patriot', you were a 'communist', and to be seen as such meant that others might decide that you deserved a 'slap' for it.

During the daytime the buzz of being a 'casual' kept him hooked on the regular Saturday hunt for trouble, but his involvement in the scene was affecting him at a deeper level. As he slept, one recurring nightmare would see him walking through a city, kicking over dustbins and chanting with his mates. Then, a car with blacked-out windows would draw up alongside them, and a group of men with guns would step out. Dave would be pursued along back alleys and hear his friends screaming as they were shot. He would hide behind a bin overflowing with refuse thinking that he had escaped. The rubbish would be kicked away and he would watch a gun being put to his head. He would see the man's grin widen. Then he would see red.

The cross-town rivalry between Bristol Rovers and City was reflected in a further recurring nightmare. He would dream that he was cornered by some faceless group of Bristol City fans in a shop doorway. There they would surround him, take out a *Stanley* knife, and slash him again and again. From these and other horrific scenes he would wake up shouting and cold with sweat, as if the attacks were actually taking place.

The weekly fighting and disturbances in which he was involved also troubled his conscience. In an attempt to find some comfort, he would turn to the back section of a small red Gideon Bible he had been given at Lawrence Weston School. Here there was a guide to which verses to read when feeling lonely, afraid or guilty. By his bedside lamp, Dave would flick through the pages, run his finger under the words, and then lie back and close his eyes. Sometimes the readings would help him to rest more easily. Perhaps as a consequence of this, or something else that he could not quite put his finger on, the book held a certain sanctity for him.

Late one afternoon, he and a friend had tried the handles of car doors along a leafy residential avenue to see if there was anything inside that they could steal and sell. They wanted the cash to fund their expensive tastes in clothing and today they had struck lucky. Whilst his mate was in the front detaching the stereo system, Dave leant into the rear to unscrew the speakers. As he glanced down below him, he noticed a substantial family Bible laid on the back seat, and he was filled with a sudden, deep terror. "Put that thing back in the dashboard," he commanded. "What? Have you gone mental? I've just got it out!" his mate replied. "Do it," said Dave. He carefully slid the speakers back into position and screwed them to the panelling. He then consciously locked the door, which he had found open, pushed his mate along, and then ran off down the avenue like a striker towards the goalmouth.

Chapter Five

CAMPAIGNS ON THE CONTINENT

Dave strode through the warm water of the fountain swaying and splashing it up at his two mates Waynus and Growler. He'd been drinking *Southern Comfort* and bottles of lager since early in the day, and now he was completely smashed.

It was the very first evening of a two-week holiday in the tourist town of Callela on the Costa Brava, and he and a crowd of English lads had gathered after pub closing time to sing 'God Save the Queen' in the town centre. They were letting any other young men within earshot know that they were English and proud of it. The local police were listening and watching, however, and they were less than impressed. One irritated officer sauntered over, took out his gun, and prodded Growler with it.

"No swear," he ordered. "No swear." Growler pushed him away.

"Get lost," spat Dave. It was enough for the policeman. He ordered all three of them out of the water and into the back seat of his patrol car. As they drove through the streets past the luminescent pub and Fish 'n' Chips shop signs, Dave thought that the driver looked like a Mexican bandit with his thin moustache and greasy, black hair.

"Hey, gringo. Hey, greeeengo," he taunted with a nasal sneer. He was having a great time, but the officer was not amused. He sneered back and slammed his radio mouthpiece into Dave's nose. Dave was too drunk to feel the pain.

At the station, only Dave and Waynus were shunted together into the dirty cell: Growler had jumped from the car on route and successfully made a run for it. Now, two dishevelled Frenchmen sat looking up at them both very nervously. Dave nodded to them, collapsed across a wooden bench, and promptly fell asleep.

Some time later when he came to, Waynus was punching one of the Frenchmen. He had seen them trying to loosen Dave's expensive *Aquascutum* shirt, and assumed they were trying to steal it. They had in fact been trying to loosen it; Dave had been choking on his vomit. In the noise of the scuffle the police arrived. They too were worried about Dave. He was passing in and out of consciousness with a bloodied nose that they had given him. They drove him as swiftly as they could to a hospital.

When Dave awoke, he was handcuffed naked to a hospital bed with a rubber tube stuffed down his throat. He was surrounded by a huddle of nurses and policemen who were attempting to pump his stomach. In sudden panic at the scene, he thrashed around and pulled out the tube. A policeman struck him with his truncheon. The nurses pushed the man back. Waynus, who was handcuffed to a nearby chair, jumped angrily into the fray. He was beaten off by the police. A needle was pushed into Dave's arm and sleep drifted through his limbs and covered his eyes.

Later, when he awoke again, his hands had been uncuffed. He rubbed his wrists to soothe them, looked around and decided to try to escape. He yanked off a bed sheet for clothing. He shouted over to Waynus, who picked up the chair that he was still cuffed to, and they ran along the ward. Patients sat up and stared at the sight as they scampered past their beds. In the hospital's entrance hall they ran straight back into the police. The Spaniards shook their heads and pointed back into the wards with their revolvers.

After they had paid their hospital bill and taken a verbal warning, they were allowed to remain in Callela. The officer's words made little impression. Dave was twenty-one years old, and it was his first outing to the continent.

On many evenings during the week, he and the English lads in the town would gather amongst the dingy décor and boxing memorabilia of the 'Golden Gloves' pub. Here the music was pitched directly to the clientele: rousing football songs and British pop anthems. Soon they would be singing and dancing on the tables, and the proprietors would keep on serving the beer. Then the locals would come to watch the English performing like animals in a freak show.

The feeling amongst the lads was that if others thought they were animals, then they would behave accordingly. The drinks would keep on flowing, they would bounce harder and higher on the tables until they collapsed, and then their glasses would start shattering on the walls.

In Callela and other destinations that Dave would travel to, he and other English 'boys' would always seek out the 'foreign opposition'. If a group of German, Dutch or French lads were pinpointed as well, all the better. Dave felt a particular loathing for these nationalities.

Often they would begin the contest by singing songs recounting British war victories, or taunt them with general abuse about their nation. Something might be thrown at them; someone might walk over and punch one; then the fight would break out.

In the July of 1990, Dave flew out to Italy to watch England's World Cup matches against Cameroon and Germany. After meeting up with his Bristol friends in the town of Sorrento, they took the train northwards to Turin for the highly anticipated semi-final.

Hundreds of conscripts in the Italian police, the Caribinieri, lined the railway station platforms at Naples in anticipation of trouble with the England fans. As the train rolled through the city the mayhem erupted. Windows were smashed, seats were thrown out, and a fire was started on board by one group of fans before another group stamped it out.

Dave joined in with a mixture of thrill and unease. Rumours were also circulating on board the train that the Juventus fans, Turin's home team, were looking for revenge for those who had died when a wall collapsed recently on spectators at the Heysel Stadium. Trouble was expected in the north.

In the city of Turin, Dave was herded along with thousands of others into the Juventus women's football club to pitch his tent for the night. The authorities wanted to contain the England supporters, and were restricting their outside access. As the evening wore on, they began to feel restless and caged up. Dave sauntered around the perimeter fence with his Bristol mates looking for a possible place to sneak out and stretch his legs. A hundred metres beyond the compound, they spotted a small group of England supporters heading towards the camp entrance. A white *Fiat* pulled up alongside them. The doors were flung open. A group of Italian youths jumped out and began to beat the young men in full view. Dave yanked fiercely at the meshing to see if he could pull it down. Others who had seen the incident joined in, hanging and swinging on the wire to force their way through. When they ran back and spread the word, the mood in the camp turned to anger.

Groups of England fans sprinted and jumped at the fences forcing an exit hole. Outside a police car drew up, but quickly reversed at high speed with its doors wide open as they charged after it. Shortly, police reinforcements began to arrive, and Dave retreated along with the others back inside the camp.

Here, one group of lads began kicking down walls and hurling the debris over the fence at the police units. The windscreen of a patrol car buckled in a spider's web of cracks as a brick struck it. Running battles between the England fans and police now spiralled on into the evening. A tractor was set ablaze and sent careering out of the compound at them. From high on a floodlight mast the glare was turned down on the ranks of Caribinieri who had gathered to push the fans back inside. The English lads aimed their missiles by it. Dave picked up a chunk of stone and swung it up over the fence. He felt both exhilarated and afraid.

A cracking noise shot through the air and small metal canisters bounced into the camp. Clouds of teargas drifted amongst the thousands of young men shouting and standing and running at the fences. The smoke swirled up into Dave's eyes. His face was burning and he gasped for breath. He jogged away and sat beneath a tree to recover his breathing, and then wandered around past the burning tents and the blue lights of the police cars watching the mayhem unfold. Later, he crawled into his tent to escape from it all.

In the early hours of the morning, his friend nudged him as he entered. "What a night Dave, and it's still going off! Not a bad birthday present for you either, eh?" he said enthusiastically.

Dave thought about it for a while. He wasn't so sure.

On the day of the semi-final of England versus Germany, Dave looked out over the vastness of Turin's Delle-Alpi stadium. The milling heads of the thousands of red, white and blue shirted England supporters swept down towards the immaculate green pitch below him.

Around the curve of the stands the shouts and chants of the mass of gathered humanity rose into a roar that was electric. Dave, though, was sitting amongst the German fans. It was an historic day, he had thought, and it deserved a deed to accompany the occasion. Shortly before play began, he glanced over at two of his Bristol friends, Popey and Percy, and two other Grimsby Town boys.

The group then stood up together. With only designer clothing to identify them, they made their way unnoticed down through the rows of German supporters to the bottom of the upper tier, and peered over the barrier railing at the heads of the England fans below. From inside his jacket Dave pulled out a St George Cross flag with Bristol Rovers written across it in large black lettering. Popey whipped out a twelve-foot Union Jack.

Quickly, Dave shoulder-barged a German youth to one side and together they flipped their colours out into the air. The flags unfurled and floated smoothly down over a draped red, yellow and black flag of the German nation. Dave hooked his sections fast and spun around.

The German fans swore and protested, but no one stepped forward to fight over it. Dave and the other boys bullishly stood their ground. The England fans below applauded. It was a further ten minutes before the police came, one of them jabbing Dave in the leg with the barrel of his revolver as they were escorted out. Back amongst the England fans, Dave held his arms aloft like a player who'd hammered home a winning goal, and they all soaked up the glory. It was a first-class sortie into foreign territory.

His sense of victory lasted a little over two hours, however, before turning to desolation. Down on the pitch, the Germans took the lead in the fifty-ninth minute; England equalised in the eightieth. Mid-fielder Paul Gascoigne famously cried his tears as he received his second yellow card of the competition, and after running into extra time, England lost the match in a penalty shoot out when Chris Waddle's shot sailed over the bar. The Germans went berserk, but the England fans fell silent. They had come so close to the final to lose in such a fashion. Dave stood looking down at his training shoes and cigarette stubs, feeling as bereft as if he had lost a family member.

The England supporters filed disconsolately away outside the stadium towards the nearby tram terminus. Dave was shunted by the police, along with his Bristol friends and forty others, despite their protestations, on a tram to the wrong terminal for their onward journey. As it slowed into the Porta Susa station, a clammy chill came over him. Through the windows on one side of the train he could see a large crowd of Juventus fans; on the other side there were hundreds of Germans. As the tram shunted to a halt and the engine cut out, the Caribinieri ordered them off. No one moved.

The situation outside was like Dunkirk. The police insisted and drew out their batons, striking home a few random blows to emphasise their point. One lad yelped as he took a whack across his legs. There was a sudden scramble for the exits. Outside the tram, a group boys from a Portsmouth 'firm' known as '657' shouted out to the rest of them,

"Come on then. We're England. This is what we're here for!" The group decided to rally to it, and charged down the platform into the German supporters as they fell back.

Dave threw a few punches and danced away, beckoning with his fingers. As he ran forward again, he saw a man in the crowd pull out what looked like a black revolver. The man drew up his arm and pointed it straight at Dave. A brilliant white light shot off the end straight at his face. At the last second the flare swerved up and over his head. Suddenly he felt a sharp blow across his back. He stumbled to the floor. He rolled over and looked up. A policeman struck down at him again with his long, thin baton, this time cracking the ground beside him. Dave staggered away in retreat.

As the fighting continued, the police surrounded the England fans and struck at them wildly. When a camera crew from the BBC scampered into the frame, the police ceased the beating and began to help those up who they had badly floored. Ambulances arrived at the scene and the police now helped the injured across. Dave sat in the rear of one of the vehicles looking blearily at a paramedic. His back was mottled yellow and purple with bruises.

After Dave returned from the World Cup tournament in Italy, he continued to attend Bristol Rovers and England matches on home soil. It was a further two years, however, before he travelled abroad to watch another England away game. This was the England versus Sweden match in Stockholm during the European Soccer Championships of 1992.

The violence that he witnessed outside the stadium; the young man being kicked repeatedly on the floor; the shock of what he himself had become a part of; and the sense of something evil and transcendent pervading the city and overpowering him in the shower blocks; all made a disturbing impression on him.

At Arlander Airport the Swedish police fingered the pages of his passport and looked him over, but they did not detain him. He caught the plane back to England, and he was thankful for the chance to turn over a new leaf himself. When he returned to Bristol, he set his mind to stay out of trouble at matches, to take a lesson from experience, and for a short while he did just that.

For some time now, Dave had been financing his lifestyle by wheeling and dealing and doing odd jobs for a contact he had made in his home city. In a not untypical job for the man, he was given three unmarked cardboard boxes to deliver. He did not want to know their contents. He placed them in the boot of his car and drove up the motorway towards Manchester. At an appointed service station a call came through on his mobile phone. He was to follow the white car parked across from him. On a nearby country lane both drivers pulled over beneath the rustling trees. Dave pressed the boot lock. The boxes were removed. A brown envelope was passed in through the window. He sped back down the motorway, returned it to his contact, and was paid £60-00 for the job.

Dave was running big risks; he was dealing with a criminal gang. When he heard whispers of guns being used to frighten people who crossed them, he decided to get away, to sever the relationship if it were possible. He arranged to leave the country for a three-week break in Thailand until things cooled down.

When he returned, his contact and some of the man's associates had been arrested.

Dave was now terrified that they would think he had something to do with it. His absence looked mightily suspicious. He felt that he would now have to constantly look over his shoulder. He was becoming ever more anxious and ill at ease.

In addition to his wheeling and dealing, Dave had developed a strong interest in alternative spiritualities. He had begun to experiment with a number of practices and read widely on dowsing, tarot and crystal healing. He was desperate for a source of inner comfort. With an interest in geology, he had made a collection of crystals and stones, and laid them on different parts of his body in an attempt to channel through supposed 'healing energies', sometimes in the hope of bringing relief to his fighting injuries.

Feeling increasingly anxious about making decisions in his life, he began to pay visits to a medium for consultations about what he should do. Regularly, he would take a thin quartz crystal on a silver chain and ask certain questions out loud. If the chain swung one way, he would do one thing, and if another, he would take a different course of action.

He had also collected a range of religious paraphernalia that he had positioned around his flat: under his bed, on the edge of his bath, and at a shrine-like focus on his night-storage heater. On the top of the TV set he kept a four inch bronze Buddha's head that he had bought in Thailand. One evening, he noticed something that left him feeling distinctly unnerved. The object was turning almost imperceptibly to face towards wherever he was sitting in his living room. Further strange and unsettling events began to happen around his flat more and more. The TV would switch itself on. Items began to disappear and then reappear in places where he would have no reason to place them. Sometimes at night he would wake up and be convinced that he had seen some indiscriminate shape moving across his bedroom. This added to the turbulence already in his sleep. His dreams were becoming bizarre and disturbing. In one recurring scene, he would be surrounded and molested by a group of grotesque, grey-skinned creatures.

Dave was finding it hard to sleep for other reasons too. Often as he lay awake in the early hours of the morning with the bedside light on and the sheets twisted around his limbs, scenes from his childhood would roam over his mind. He was angry with everyone who had ever picked on him, put him down or misunderstood him. He thought about the teacher who had pushed him into the mud, about his father for cheating him out of his pocket money, about Cliff for caning him, and about his mother for losing her temper and coating him with yoghurt. He thrashed around sweating as he thought about how he had been wronged, and he grew angry with himself that he was so wound up and unable to sleep. He flipped over and struck the bedroom wall with his fist.

His desire to lash back in anger was vented on unlucky recipients; these were often the cocky and the pushy in bars. If Dave felt that someone was having a go at him, he could not turn the other cheek, and his tactics were sneaky and brutal. Placing his drink down on the table, he would walk in close, his hands held open in conciliation. The muscles in his neck would tense up, his head would rock from side to side like some Indian dancer, and then a stabbing butt would be delivered. He would then follow through with punches until the man fell.

When Dave had walked away, though, his self-satisfaction would be short-lived. Remorse would often strike him back so quickly that he would return to buy pints for his confused victim. Sometimes he would track a person down at a later date and for what it was worth apologise.

One cold April morning, Dave felt the urge to sit alone in the quiet of a church building. He had been to Salvation Army services with his mother in the past after bad fights and brushes with the police, as much for her as for anything. But today he wanted to go on his own terms, to think and maybe find some peace in his head. At a large Anglican church near his flat, Dave walked tentatively towards the building's doors up a wide stone staircase. An ageing verger suddenly appeared and began to look him over. "Can I help you?" he enquired.

"I just want to sit down inside," replied Dave.

"You can't. The building is closed," said the man curtly. Dave didn't like his attitude and he couldn't understand how a church of all things could be closed.

"Oh, right," he sneered. "Nice to be welcomed. You know what you can do with your church then, don't you?"

He spun around and left. A little further along the road, he came to a modern Catholic Cathedral with two large stone pinnacles. This time the building was open and no one was guarding the door. Dave stepped nervously inside and slid along a row of plastic seats at the rear.

In the silence he felt more at peace. He sat still and looked around. He felt that he had something to say to God, if he was here in this building, but he dare not shout it out loud. "Come on then... if you are real. Let's see it. Let's have it then... Come on!" he ranted in his head.

Dave heard a noise behind him. A woman in a fawn overcoat was placing a lit candle by a statue of Mary. Dave waited but nothing else happened. He sat for a while and then he left. Two days later he returned to the same place. "Where are you then? Where are you eh? You're a fat lot of use. Why don't you help me?" he shouted through the noise in his mind.

Dave sat and waited. Some weeks later, he walked across the grass in front of the concave council buildings and into the city's Anglican Cathedral. He sat for a while on a bench at the rear, listening to the noise of footsteps echoing across the stone paving flags. He felt angry with himself for giving any God there was in these places a further opportunity to cold-shoulder him.

"Right, this is it this time," he said under his breath with a bitter desperation. "You'd better show up, because I'm not coming back here again." As he left, he paused for a minute in a small chapel to the right of the altar. On a table there was a large brown album in which people had written their prayers. Dave took the pen and wrote in two short words.

On a rainy winter's day, events were completely on top of him. To add to everything else, he had recently split up with a girlfriend. For a while he had been living back at home with his mother and stepfather, but they could only deal with his lifestyle for so long, and had reached their limit with him again. For the second time in his life, he had been asked to leave home in three weeks time. Dave did not tell anyone what he intended to do.

He slumped into his white *Vauxhall Astra GTE,* and set off driving through the city holding the wheel with a forced determination. It was early on a Saturday afternoon, and as he drew nearer to the Ashton Gate stadium, he got caught up in the match traffic. He snivelled and laughed to himself as he drove along. How could it be that on this his last day he should be surrounded by fans from his archrival team Bristol City, 'Robins'?—their scarves flapping irritatingly from the windows of their cars. South of the city, he drove steadily towards the Mendip Hills. Close to the limestone cliffs of Cheddar Gorge, he coasted through an open gate and across a dirt field. He drew the vehicle to a halt and turned off the engine.

He sat silently, watching the rainwater snaking in lines down the windscreen. He took out a cigarette and lit it. He thought about what he was going to do. He knew that driving straight over the edge onto the road below would be as certain a way of finishing things as anyone could want.

Chapter Six

THE CANDLE
PROJECT

Dave picked up a large, steaming teapot, and filled up a line of white cups laid out on the counter. In front of him, a man wearing broken reading glasses and a creased overcoat pointed at a plate of biscuits and protested that there weren't any custard creams. Dave shrugged his shoulders. He was helping out his mother at the Salvation Army centre in the district of St Paul's serving lunch for the neighbourhood's homeless.

Somehow looking at the men and women here took away the sting of his own circumstances for an hour or two. He felt a strange kinship with them. A young West Indian girl standing awkwardly on high heels, a dwarf whose skin was purple with broken blood vessels from drinking too much alcohol: the people here had strife in their faces and were struggling just to get by.

Dave felt angry that it should be this way for anyone. In the field near Cheddar Gorge, he had thought about putting his foot on the pedal and firing himself over the edge, but when it came to the moment of acceleration, he just couldn't do it. He had spun the wheel around, sped out through the gate, and then driven sluggishly back into the city. He still had all his problems to face.

For some time now he had been volunteering here at the 'Candle Project'. His mother had encouraged him to come along and give her a hand. He knew she thought it might be a way of diverting his energies away from being a 'casual' into something positive. But he thought that he'd better be around to act as a bodyguard in case any of the visitors made trouble. He wanted to make sure that no one shoved his mum around.

Val had started 'The Candle Project' out of a deep desire to make a difference in an inner city environment. She had become a Christian and joined the Salvation Army when Dave was sixteen, and had since felt a growing calling to demonstrate love in a practical way amongst those on the margins of society. The project, which she herself had conceived and set in motion, aimed to provide useful facilities and support specifically for the area's homeless. The red brick centre had been fitted with showers and a washing machine for visitors to use. A medical room with a visiting doctor and nurse on hand once a week had been organised. Regular hot meals were cooked up in the kitchen. A rota of volunteers chatted and spent time with anyone who wanted to talk. Val now oversaw the centre and made herself available to offer advice and links with other agencies and professionals concerned with the visitors' welfare. The atmosphere at the 'Candle' was organised, warm and welcoming.

Dave admired the work that his mother was doing, and his concern for her safety was not without foundation. Most of the visitors to 'Candle' abused drugs or alcohol, some had mental health issues, and many displayed challenging anti-social behaviour.

There was a need for security, even if Dave's methods were to prove a little rough. On one occasion, an alcoholic, a wiry ex-miner with a reputation for causing trouble, began picking on another visitor. Val asked him to leave. He refused and began shouting back obscenities. When Dave repeated the request, he spat out a mouth full of onions in his face. Dave felt a surge of anger at the foulness of the insult. He could not hold back his reflexes, and he head butted the man before punching him twice. Other volunteers pulled back his arms to stop him beating the man further.

Shortly, Dave shuffled around on a chair in the kitchen and looked uncomfortably up at the other workers. He felt pretty disgusted with himself. He knew it was hardly the treatment visitors expected from the Salvation Army, even if he were just a volunteer.

On a further occasion, a drunken man in a distressed state began running a knife across his face and drawing blood. Dave grasped the man by the arm and throat to restrain him, and they began to wrestle together. Val tried to pull them apart, grabbing Dave by the hair and shouting at him to let the man go. When the scuffle broke up, Dave was turfed out of the centre.

Val was furious with his strong-arm tactics. He skulked around for a few days; he had only been trying to look after her. It wasn't long, however, before he was back again at the centre, pouring out teas and hoisting the heavy pans of soup across the kitchen. On other occasions, a couple of

Dave's mates from football came down to the 'Candle' to volunteer. In truth they had been in trouble with the police, and thought they might get a reference out of working here. They too would have little truck with abusive alcoholics, and when word got around that the Salvation Army had bouncers at their Sunday dinner, behaviour amongst some of the visitors noticeably improved.

At the end of the opening sessions at 'Candle', many of the volunteers would pull their chairs together into a circle and pray out loud as if God were present in the room. Dave watched them from a distance, and sometimes listened in as they petitioned Him in prayer on behalf of one of the homeless visitors. Even though he had himself entered churches alone and ranted up at God in his head, he felt little desire to join them. It seemed to him that they were oblivious of what was really going on in the world. He thought they were laughably naïve.

"Come and join us Dave," they would invite him regularly. There was something about their open friendliness that bugged him.

"No thanks," he'd reply. "If you lot really care about the homeless, then they'd be better off if you got up off your rear ends instead of sitting around talking into space."

He went about his business, sweeping up the kitchen floor or chatting with anyone else who wanted his company.

One Tuesday afternoon in the July of 1995, Dave noticed a new volunteer laying the tables in the centre's dining area. Gabby was a small, bubbly girl who had just completed the final year of her degree at Bristol University. Though students were not Dave's favourite social group, having quickly taken a shine to her, he decided to make an exception. He invited Gabby out for a coffee, and he could sense that she liked him too. After two weeks of meeting up at the 'Candle', Dave decided he wanted to take the relationship further.

Gabby, however, put the brakes on. She explained to Dave that because she was a Christian and he wasn't, she didn't want to get seriously involved with him. Dave was not going to be put off that easily; he figured he could win her over anyway. The next time they met, he asked her out for a drink.

"Okay Dave," she replied. "I'll come with you, if you come with me to the church service before we go."

Dave thought about it. He was none too happy about the condition, but he figured it was an inconvenience worth the payoff.

Dave began to feel distinctly ill at ease when he entered the building of Bristol

Community Church. There seemed to be something in the air of the place that made him feel restless and agitated. He looked around at the grinning pastor shaking hands with the congregation, at the child-like, embroidered banners hanging from the walls, and at the neat chairs packed annoyingly tight together. He noticed a group of younger men and marked them down as students by their clothing. The people were speaking without a Bristol accent.

It's a bit posh here, he thought. Others were eyeing him up and down, and he felt that everyone could see he was a newcomer. If they don't like what they see, they know what they can do, he said to himself. He sat down on a hard chair at the end of a row. He figured that he could get out easily here if he'd had enough. He glanced across at Gabby and imagined a long, cool glass of lager waiting shortly on the top of an oak pub table.

When the service got underway, he did not know the words to the songs and he was none too impressed with the melodies. He stared at the passing sheets on the overhead projector and looked down at his watch. Half way through the service, a time for prayer was announced, and the congregation coughed and shuffled as they settled into the silence.

Dave sat uncomfortably with his thoughts. He didn't want to be here, and he glanced over at the exit. He thought about his nightmares. He thought about how he had sent the black snooker ball spinning through the air at the Luton Town fan's forehead, and how he had been beaten on the bus to Lawrence Weston School.

He put his hands up to his eyes and covered his face. He didn't want to think. When he pulled them away, there were tears running over the palms of his hands: he couldn't believe it. He wiped them furtively across his thighs and looked across at Gabby.

He got to his feet and strode quickly to the door of the church. Outside on the concrete paving flags, he pulled out his packet of cigarettes. He tapped one out, lit it up, and drew deeply, turning the box in his fingers and glancing anxiously back at the church door. Gabby came running out with a questioning look in her eyes. Dave was breathing heavily.

"What's the matter Dave?" she said.

"Nothing. Really. It's nothing."

"Are you sure?"

"Yes I'm sure," he snapped. "I just didn't like it in there with all those people."

Later, in a pokey student pub close to the University, Dave sat looking down into the lines of bubbles rising up through his fifth pint of lager. He felt removed now from the day's events. Gabby had left him after the first couple of drinks, and he felt warm and at home here.

He thought about the service and the way it had churned him up. "There's no way I'm going back there," he said under his breath. "No fear."

When Dave saw Gabby again, she invited him to a further meeting at the church the following Tuesday evening. "Will you come with me Dave?" she enquired.

He didn't have to think about it for long. "Er, thanks Gabby, but I think I'll give it a miss this time," he said coolly.

"What's the matter? Are you scared?" she replied.

Dave felt suddenly annoyed at the suggestion: it was laughable. He had climbed over the fence into the away fans at the Rovers ground with just a couple of other 'boys'. He was not going to let anyone think that he was scared of attending a church service. "Alright then," he replied defiantly, "I'll see you there."

Dave sat well away from the front on the following Tuesday evening. He did not feel any more at ease for having been here once before. He muttered an occasional song lyric during the service so he would not appear any more out of place than he felt. He looked around at the rows of worshippers, all of who seemed to be singing over-enthusiastically, or drifting with their eyes closed on their own internal journey. He ran his hand across his forehead, and around the collar of his shirt. He hated it here and he wanted to get out as fast as he could. He looked to his left and right but he felt trapped in the middle of a row of people. Some of them were looking at him.

Then he felt the backs of his eyes begin to smart. It was happening again. What was it about this place? He was determined to contain himself. He clenched his fists and tried to fight the tears back. He covered his face with his hands, but his shoulders began to shake. He rocked forward to rest his face on his knees and sat upright taking a deep breath. He could not keep his feelings in, and he brushed his cheeks with his shirtsleeve.

Two young men approached him along the aisle. He eyed them up and down. "Can we pray for you?" one of them asked quietly.

"You can do whatever you want," he replied with a thinly concealed hostility.

"Well what do YOU want?" one of the young men replied.

Dave thought about it for a moment. He remembered the Gillingham 'boy' with the blue *Kickers* shoes booting him in the head on the chip shop floor, and the fallen man outside the stadium in Stockholm, and his nights striking the bedroom wall with his fist. He felt as if his mind was flitting around for a haven like some injured gull on a beach of oil pools.

"I don't know. I just want it all to go… what I feel inside," he said slowly.

"Will you hold out your hands to receive?" said one young man.

Dave stood up. He looked squarely at the two young men. "What are you going to do about it, magic it all away?" he scoffed.

He half heard them say something about Christ, but he was already cupping his hands upwards. He closed his eyes. He felt so hungry for something. Suddenly, his legs began to give way at the knees, as if someone was laying him down to rest.

Dave looked steadily around him when he came to. He was sprawled on the floor of the church, with a number of the chairs scattered around him like topped traffic cones. Gabby was sitting next to him. The two young men were smiling down at him. He felt a new sensation all through his body. His muscles were relaxed, his mind was still, and the ache in his heart had eased. He felt like the straps of some invisible rucksack had slipped away from his shoulders, and that somehow the things that he had once done were no longer of importance. He righted a chair and sat across it.

Gabby was smiling now at him too. He felt like smiling. He knew that what had happened had come from outside of himself. He knew that this was God. He knew that he had been touched by God. He shook his head and laughed in disbelief and astonishment.

"All these years... All these years..." he said quietly. "I don't believe it. The Man Upstairs, he's flipping real." He smiled at Gabby, and then nodded reluctantly at the two students.

For the next couple of days, Dave felt as if he were on such a high that he wondered if it could last. At his flat, he snatched repeatedly at the receiver of his telephone and dialled his mother's number. He desperately wanted to tell her about what had happened. She was away on her holidays, but he knew she would be back any time now. He dialled and redialled her hourly, but each time he heard the ring tone repeat on and on.

Eventually, the receiver was lifted. "Hello mum... Are you sitting down?" he shouted, relieved and excited. There was a tense silence. He knew that she would be expecting him to ask her to bail him out of some dire circumstance. He knew that she had been praying for him for eleven years. "I just thought that you'd like to know... I became a Christian this week..."

For a few moments more there was silence, then Dave could hear her sobbing.

Chapter Seven

SWORD FOR THE FIGHT

As Dave drove his car on a hot, pollen-heavy day the following week to his first ever Christian camp, 'Soul Survivor', he thought about the advice his mother had given him. Immediately after the Tuesday prayer meeting, he had come under pressure from people in the church to stop doing one thing and to start doing another. He was feeling deeply stressed about it all. At this moment in time, he didn't feel confident that he knew his right hand from his left any more; he felt a little like a bewildered infant. His mother had told him to take everything step by step, and that God would show him the right time. It made him feel a little easier.

On his first evening at the Royal Bath and West Show Ground in Somerset, where thousands of Christians gather each summer for four days of teaching, worship and ministry, things did not go so smoothly. After Gabby departed to sample the program, Dave produced a large crate of French beers from the car boot, took out his packet of cigarettes, and settled in for a normal evening's relaxation by his tent. Shortly, an earnest young man in a bright steward's vest approached him. "What do you think you are doing? This is an alcohol-free festival," he protested indignantly.

Dave told him to take a long walk. After other church members repeated the request, he reluctantly lowered the crate back into the boot of his car. Later in the evening, when a nearby youth group began singing enthusiastically, he strode over and gave them a mouthful of abuse. How could anyone hope to sleep with such a holy racket going on? The teenagers stared back with their mouths wide open. When he returned to camp, he could sense that the people at Gabby's church were becoming very uneasy with him.

At eleven o' clock that evening, Gabby herself made the decision that they weren't the ideal match, and told him that she was calling things off. Dave yanked up the pegs of his tent and repitched it away in the corner of the field. He'd had enough of this place and these people. He decided he was going to pack up and go back to Bristol in the morning.

Dave threw his equipment on to the back seat of his car the next day. When he tried to turn the ignition key, though, it was as if he physically couldn't bring himself to do it. He tried to turn the key again, but something inside prevented him. He fought to twist it past the steering lock one more time, and then slammed his fist into the dashboard. He just wanted to go home, get drunk with his mates and have a fight, and it was as if he was being prevented from leaving.

"Why won't you let me go?" he shouted up at God. "I know you want me to stay, but I don't want to. Let me go…" He sat for a while breathing heavily, his head resting on the centre of the steering wheel. Reluctantly, he pulled the door handle, swung his legs out, and made his way sluggishly back towards the church tents.

As he attended the teaching seminars and services over the next couple of days, however, he began to warm to the event. He found the talks on the Bible enlightening, and after each of the times of worship, when there was an opportunity for people to walk forward and be prayed for, Dave stepped up to receive all that he could get. In a growing zeal, he was struck with a sense of righteous indignation when he learnt of the presence of a reputed Satanist at the gathering. Dave decided that he would find him and sort him out. Such people, bad people, he reasoned, deserved a 'slap'.

In the gentlemen's toilets he came across his opportunity. The man had a long, knobbly walking staff, which he had leant against the urinal wall. Dark make up arched around his eyes and a selection of inverted crucifixes hung around his neck. Dave looked at his strange quarry with contempt. He walked across slowly to him.

"So, what's all this then?" he said, pointing to the man's jewellery. The man regarded him coolly. "What are you doing here?" said Dave. The man grinned back with half of his mouth and made a clever remark.

"Come on then," said Dave, beckoning with his fingers. "Do you want some?" Dave wanted to snap his walking staff, but others by the hand-dryers stepped in to prevent the assault. An older man led Dave away to one side.

"This is perhaps not the best way to tackle the man, is it?" he said quietly. Dave nodded. He looked back at the man, and left the toilets feeling awkward with himself. Despite this incident, 'Soul Survivor' ended on a higher note for him. On the last day, without ever anticipating he could do such a thing, he stepped up onto the stage before the thousands of gathered worshippers, and talked about his involvement in football hooliganism and what God was beginning to do in his life.

Back in Bristol, Dave did not quite feel at ease attending Bristol Community church, so he was grateful for a further suggestion from his mother. Shortly after returning from the summer camp, he began to go along to Henleaze and Westbury Community Church, a growing inner-city fellowship with a large number of young people that was part of a wider community known as Woodlands Church.

The pastor at Henleaze, Dave Mitchell, a gently spoken man with long, dark hair, soon made Dave feel welcome. He and his wife Tina lived just around the corner from Dave's flat near Clifton's Georgian terraces, and he began to spend many hours at his new pastor's house, turning up for tea with his Bible to question him about the meaning of different verses. Dave felt warmly welcomed here, and his interest in the stories of God's works, especially amongst the Hebrew wars in the books of Joshua and Kings, was fed and encouraged by Dave and Tina.

For the first time in his life, he felt he understood the actual Christian significance of Easter and Christmas, in contrast to the holiday and present swapping festival he had always taken them to be. He learnt that he was loved by God, and that he had been forgiven for the things he had done because he had asked for it. It seemed an amazing mystery to him, but he felt it, and he believed it to be so.

The Henleaze community met in a disused Victorian School building, and held two services on a Sunday morning and one in the evening. Dave went along enthusiastically to all of them. The other members of the church were kind and welcoming to him, and even though he felt there was no one else from his background in the congregation, he felt a little more at home with them.

After one particular service, Dave felt that it was time to make amends for many of the items he had furnished his flat with over the years. Some of the pictures on his living room walls had been snatched from pubs when fighting had broken out and the landlord's attention had been distracted. Much of his electronic equipment—his TV, video recorder, hi-fi and washing machine—had been obtained through some dodgy, back street deal. He also still had the odd designer shirt, snatched from an Italian shopping mall when he and other England 'boys' had stormed through on the rampage. Dave decided that he did not wish to keep such things any more, and that he would give them all away.

As he prayed about what he should do with them, he would regularly get a strong sense in his heart of an individual he knew who needed such an item. He would then give each thing as a gift to them. Though not a perfect means of redressing each offence, he felt it was a restitution of a kind. In a further purging of his possessions, he gathered up his 'healing' crystals, his Malaysian monkey god plaques, and his bronze Buddha's head, and lay them outside in the car park at the rear of his flat. Then, with a three-pound lump hammer he pummelled them into buckled discs and powder, 'bosh', 'thwack', against the hard concrete surface. He tore up a substantial selection of his books and burnt them there too. As he glanced away from the little cluster of flames at the windows of the flats above him, he could see his neighbours' curtains swing back into position. They probably think I've lost the plot, he smirked to himself.

On many evenings during his first month at the church as he lay in bed at night, and on other occasions later, he would feel a gentle prompting inside to rid himself of a further item he was keeping. Sometimes he would hand it on to someone a couple of days later, other nights he would pull on his dressing gown and training shoes there and then, and return to the car park with his lump hammer.

As Dave surveyed his now sparsely furnished home, he began to experience signs of a special presence providing for him. One morning, as he wondered about how he would find the money to pay his current electricity bill, he heard his letter box snap shut. When he opened an unmarked white envelope lying on the doormat, he found the exact amount of cash he needed to meet the payment. He opened the front door and peered both ways down the street, but he could not see the person who'd delivered it. He had told no one about the bill. He fingered the crisp notes and thought about it. At first he felt a little unnerved, but then a warm sense of delight and awe came over him. Could it really be that God had prompted someone in the church to give him the money?

On a number of occasions over the following months, he found envelopes of notes pushed under his door for the living expenses he was struggling to meet. Though he knew that certain people in the congregation were helping him, the timing and the quantities being delivered, without him speaking requests to anyone, gave him a deepening sense that God was not simply out there at a distance, but present with him in his flat.

Not long after he had begun attending the services at Henleaze church, and thrown out his collection of religious objects, Dave began to sleep more easily at nights. The nightmares about being attacked began to wane, and were replaced by nocturnal scenes of a different character. One dream left a deep impression on him. As he walked along an ordinary, suburban avenue, he heard God's voice tell him not to enter a particular bed and breakfast house. "I can take good care of myself Lord", he replied.

As he lay down on his bed to sleep, four devilish creatures entered and began laughing at him. When he shouted at them to leave, they sniggered derisively. They then climbed onto the bed and began to molest him. He kicked and punched and head butted them, but they continued the assault until he ordered them in the name of Jesus to stop.

'You're not sure, are you? You don't really have the authority to say that, do you?' they replied. As Dave doubted himself, they sprung back at him again. At that point, the door opened and light fell into the room. Dave could see an angel with a Roman helmet concealing its eyes holding a bow and arrow. The angel raised its arm and the terrified creatures fled in an instant.

Dave cried out, "I'm sorry. I'm sorry. I should have listened." The angel then took him by the hand, and led him through the light of the doorway. When Dave awoke, he looked around the darkness of his bedroom. He felt calm but his thoughts were racing. The meaning of the dream was clear to him: God did speak to people, and he should pay real heed to what was said to him.

When Dave lay in his bed at night trying to sleep on a further occasion, he began to feel a certain fear of the dark presence he had experienced many times before in his flat. A film of cold sweat formed on his forehead and his neck muscles tightened. He clenched his fists, but he still felt exposed and vulnerable. As he lay looking around him, he thought he heard a calm, audible voice tell him to read the Bible's 91st Psalm. Dave flicked the bedside light switch, and thumbed through the pages until he found it. Verses 4-6 read:

> He will cover you with his feathers, and under his wings you will find refuge. His faithfulness will be your shield and your rampart. You will not fear the terror of the night, nor the arrow that flies by day, nor the pestilence that stalks in the darkness.

He was amazed. The verses seemed so specifically relevant. Whatever darkness might still remain in his home, he felt that he was being given God's personal assurance of His protection from it. He felt a calmness settle over him, and he did not experience the dark presence in his flat again. Though he had taken to reading the Bible on a daily basis, there were still huge sections of it, including the Psalms, that he hadn't yet looked at.

He did not find reading any books easy. On this and many other occasions, verse references surfaced in his mind from what seemed obscure Old and New Testament books. He would look them up and find they had an uncanny relevance to the feelings and situations he was struggling with. In a further time of deep uncertainty about what he might do with his life in the future, he felt prompted to read a passage from the book of Jeremiah.

> 'For I know the plans I have for you,' declares the Lord, 'plans to prosper you and not to

harm you, plans to give you a hope and a future.'

[Chapter 29:11]

This too gave him a strength and confidence, even though he could not see ahead to any tangible opportunities in his life.

Even though Dave felt a deep desire to grow in his knowledge and understanding of God, and it would seem like almost every day he would see some sign of His presence with him, attending church services felt regularly like an unbearable struggle.

As the worship songs and times of prayer got underway at Henleaze, he would feel a powerful urge to stand up and hurl obscenities at everyone, or to throw chairs around the room and lash out in anger. Sometimes he would have to take himself out of the hall to avoid causing a scene; so much of his inner world felt turbulent and tormented.

Often, as he sat looking at the service leaders leaning into the microphone stands, a chain of thought told him that he did not belong in the church, that the people here hated him, and that he would be best served in the long term by getting as far away from them as possible.

Dave hung on in his head to the knowledge that as far as God was concerned he was accepted and forgiven for the things that he had done: for the mayhem and the violence and the damage to both others and himself. Weekly, he would confess how he felt to those who remained after the service, and their regular prayers seemed to calm him little by little.

On other occasions, the results of such times of prayer would be far more dramatic. When Dave Mitchell prayed for him, he sometimes could not look him in the eyes. His mind would seem suddenly choked up with malicious thoughts, and he would shout out swearing and cursing everyone present. Then, as he panted and gasped for air, he would feel released of something noxious that was churning him up inside. Afterwards, he would lie back across the hall chairs, and rest for a while in a warm sense of peace that would regularly envelop him. Dave knew that God was now at work changing him steadily from the inside out, but it seemed like such a slow and difficult process.

He asked Dave Mitchell about it. "Why can't it all just happen at once?"

"Because you would be little more than a blob Dave," he replied. "So much of what we hold on to in ourselves would be taken away."

The sight of grown people skipping along the aisles waving banners during worship was a source of annoyance and embarrassment to Dave. In addition to the battle he felt within, the culture of the church often seemed like an alien environment. He secretly wanted to snap their little flags. He also struggled with the congregation's taste for the softer, intimate, guitar-led worship songs; he warmed to the more traditional and robust. One hymn, 'Be Thou My Vision', came to have a powerful significance for him. It reflected his daily reality, his hopes and his inner conflicts.

> Be Thou my vision, O Lord of my heart
> Be all else but naught to me, save that Thou art
> Be thou my best thought in the day and the night
> Both waking and sleeping, Thy presence my light.
>
> Be Thou my wisdom, be Thou my true word
> Be Thou ever with me, and I with Thee, Lord
> Be Thou in me dwelling, and I with Thee one
> Be Thou my great Father, and I Thy true son.
>
> Be Thou my breastplate, my sword for the fight
> Be Thou my whole armour, be Thou my true might
> Be Thou my soul's shelter, be Thou my strong tower
> Oh raise Thou me heavenward, great Power of my power.

Though he could see that the worship style was just a superficial issue, at the same time it made it harder for him to relax into the order of things.

Dave's mum occasionally took an evening off from her services at the Salvation Army in St Paul's to come along with him to his church. One time, as all other seating was taken, Dave sat in the row behind her and watched as she sat pensively through the sermon and the time of prayer.

He'd felt so angry with her for siding with his stepfather, for not understanding him, and for throwing him out of the house. But somehow now he felt that he could let it go. He was struck afresh by how she had always been there for him, and how much she must have been through because of the trouble he'd been in at school, at football matches, and when he'd been out drinking with his mates. He couldn't believe how lucky he was to have her as a mother—and Cliff as a stepfather for that matter.

At the end of the service, she came and sat next to him. He could see the water welling in her eyes. She put her arms around him and held him. Dave lay his head on her shoulder and held on to her arms. He could not keep back his tears, and his muscles shook as he held her tighter than he could ever remember having done before. It seemed to him like a wall that had been there between them was crumbling away. It felt so good. He sensed that this too must be God's work: it was such an amazing and wonderful thing.

When the football season began again in the autumn, Dave walked back along the terraces at the Memorial Ground to join his mates. It felt good to be back amongst the fans, the 'gas', singing the club song 'Good-night Irene' as it caught on in waves across the crowd, shouting down encouragement at the Rovers players on the pitch, as well as mocking the opposition's goal keeper. He loved the atmosphere and the banter and the familiar smell of pasties from the ground's kiosks. Though some of his friends had heard the news about what had happened to him over the summer, he was going to break it to others for the first time. He did not intend to keep it a secret; he wanted everyone to know what a difference it had made in his life.

"It's like this... I've become a Christian," he explained. There were one or two bemused glances.

"What... like one of them born again Christians?" said one lad with a crew cut.

"Yeah, I guess so," Dave replied.

"Come on Dave. You must be getting something out of the church? What's the scam?" said a stocky looking scaffolder.

"You're stitching them up for something, aren't you? He's a right one, isn't he? Fleecing the flippin' church now, he is!" said another lad, slapping his mate across the arm and pointing at Dave with a knowing smile.

"Nah. I'm not, it's for real," replied Dave. He held his eyes on them without grinning. No one knew how to reply. There was a round feeling of uncertainty about Dave's latest announcement.

In the nearby Duke of Wellington pub after the match, the teasing began. "Are you sure it's okay to have a pint now, Jesus?" said the lad with the crew cut.

"Are you going to swap your clobber for a Caftan then?" another lad chipped in, and everyone fell about laughing.

Dave answered back with his own banter, giving as good as he got. He hung around for a while, listening in and laughing along with the conversation until he'd finished his pint, but the jokes were beginning to smart. Feeling one step outside of the circle, he finished off his pint, zipped up his jacket, and nodded around the group. He knew that his life was forking away from theirs, and a feeling of sadness came over him.

Trouble kicked off on the terraces a couple of weeks later when Rotherham United came to Bristol and the away fans showed up in the Rovers end. Dave felt the same old surge of adrenaline. This was an incursion onto his turf that should rightly be seen off. He wanted to run and jump into the fray, but he held himself back. As some of his mates ducked under the hand railings and jogged towards the scuffling crowds, he felt a growing sensation of sickness at the spectacle. He felt as if he was watching it now through a clean pair of glasses. It unsettled him and he wanted to look away. He turned his thoughts on to himself.

Chapter Eight

DOWN AND OUT IN DURBAN

When Dave answered the telephone at his Clifton flat later in the autumn, he could not have anticipated how the conversation to follow would open up such an unimagined opportunity.

"You don't know me," said the man in an unusual accent, "but I know about you." For a moment, fear flickered through him as he wondered who on earth this person might be. "How would you like to come and work with us in South Africa?" the man continued.

Dave was astonished, and also considerably relieved. At the previous Sunday morning service at Henleaze, a visiting team of South African church workers had spoken about their mission amongst the homeless in the city of Durban. Dave had paid little attention to the presentation; it had all seemed too far removed from his concerns. He told the man he was a little surprised, but that he would think it over.

"By the way, how did you get my number?" he asked, still a little wary.

"The Lord works in mysterious ways," the man replied.

'Oh yes?' thought Dave.

A couple of days later, Dave drove with his mother to a large Victorian house in an affluent suburb of the city. There he met two South African pastors, who spelt out the details of the invitation over tea and a plate of biscuits. If he wanted to take up their offer, he would be welcome to stay at The Ark, an old seaman's mission building close to Durban's docks, where he could help out amongst the homeless residents. Dave thought about the work that he'd been doing with his mother at the Candle Project, and what a good experience it might be for him.

He wanted to try it, but there was the serious issue of money. He needed to pay for the flight and then have enough for his living expenses. At the moment, he had barely a spare five-pound-note. There was also the matter of his Council Tax bill, which he had neglected to pay for a very long time prior to the summer.

Late that evening, he sat with his back on the bed's headboard, and prayed out loud: "Lord, if you want me to go to South Africa, then you're going to have to provide the money!" Then, he shuffled under the sheets and flicked the bedside lamp switch.

The following morning, a small white envelope was waiting for him on his doormat. It contained £50-00 in crisp notes. Dave smiled right through to his soul. It seemed to him that this was a clear sign that a stay in Durban was now the thing to do. Over the following two weeks, the money flowed in. Members of his church and family gave him more than enough to clear his debts, and then added sufficient to make the whole excursion possible.

When Dave arrived at the old seaman's mission building on Durban's Point Road, just two months after he had received the invitation, he thought that there had been a serious mistake. Outside, the building looked like some grim, redbrick Victorian workhouse. Inside, over a thousand of the city's homeless men and women – blacks, whites and coloureds of all ages—were bedding down below its dirty white walls. The smell of bodies and refuse fermenting like some noxious brew in the confined heat was overpowering. The washing facilities consisted of a single dribbling pipe in the wall, and buckets of hot water that the residents spooned over themselves with empty margarine tubs.

Dave was speechless. He just wanted a nice warm shower and a clean *Burberry* shirt. As the mission was unsupported by the government, the residents were praying in their food by faith every day. Deliveries of out of date stock would arrive from different donors in the city: boxes of unwanted popcorn, crates of overripe fruit, and leftovers direct from wedding ceremony banquets. When Dave sat down to a dinner of maize gruel, his appetite swiftly left him. The Ark was not even fit for Noah's animals, he thought. It was nothing like the Candle Project.

Dave sat in a doorless toilet cubicle, unpacked his box of two hundred duty free cigarettes, and filled the air with a heavy cloud of smoke. He wanted to catch the first flight back to London. He slipped out quietly to a nearby drinking spot, a *'shabeen'*, to get some change for the telephone. He intended to call his mother and let her know. When he produced a 500 rand note, all the drinkers followed him outside hassling him for a donation: it was more than the establishment had in the till. He was completely cornered until The Ark's security team, who had noticed his absence, arrived to make their presence known. He felt deeply relieved that someone had seen him leave.

Later that evening, he was shown to his room, which he was to share with six other homeless men. He looked down uncomfortably at his mattress; it was fusty and stained. As he tried to block out the rasping snores of the men with his fingers in the early hours, he heard gunshots outside, and then the wailing sirens of police units tearing past, shaking the building's windows with the volume.

He just couldn't believe it: it was bad enough inside, but outside it seemed as rough as some suburb of Beirut. Soon the noise of raindrops started to patter onto the broken-tiled roof. The bed began to feel cold beneath his legs. He reached down to feel a large damp patch, and then placed his hand on the wall: water was flowing down its surface. He shuffled his body to balance it on the edge of the mattress and muttered a terse prayer.

"Thanks Lord. This is just great. What for flip's sake have you led me here for?"

The bright Durban sunshine was streaming in through the windows when

Dave awoke the following morning, and his spirits lifted a little. Over the plain bread breakfast he chatted with a hefty Indian man, Des, who he'd met the previous evening. When Dave had shaken the man's hand as they were introduced, he had recoiled. Des's right-hand ring finger was missing, and he had wiggled the remaining stump on his palm. Dave learnt that the handshake was an old favourite with the man, and he warmed to him right away. Des offered to take him along on a visit to a nearby old people's home, and as they prayed with the elderly residents and got to know each other a little, it took his mind away from the previous day.

Later, after Dave protested that he was English, and couldn't live in a room with six other snorting men because he just wasn't used to it, a store cupboard was found and a camp bed laid down in it specially for him. It was a privilege that he alone enjoyed at The Ark. Dave felt a little guilty, but he was well pleased. He felt that a stay might just be endurable now for a short while.

After the meal had been cleared away from The Ark's hotchpotch of tables, every evening of the week the mission sent out a small team to walk the seafront and rundown apartment blocks of the Point Road. The group set out to talk to the homeless and help them in any way they could. Dave began to make regular excursions into the warm Durban nights with them, along with his newfound friend, Des.

Late one evening, as they walked along the beach enjoying the cool sea breeze coming in off the Indian ocean, a man came running along the water's edge towards them at a wild speed. The man was growling and yanking at his matted dreadlocks like some half-crazed shaman. Dave looked around at the other team members. There was hesitation in their eyes about what to do. Dave had learnt from Des that the practice of witchcraft was not uncommon in the area, and it seemed to him that the man was in some kind of spiritually tormented state. He knew full well how dark forces could oppress a person.

Dave decided to take a chance. As the man ran closer he stretched out his arm and pointed firmly at him. "In the name of Jesus, I command you to be quiet," he shouted. To everyone's amazement, not least Dave's, the man fell over flat in a cloud of sand. The group gathered around him as he lay looking up at them, his rib cage heaving. They prayed quietly over him, and soon the man, who said nothing by way of an explanation, was sleeping as peacefully as if he were in his mother's arms. The team made him comfortable and continued on their nightly patrol. As Dave walked away, he felt awed by what he had witnessed.

On a further evening, when Dave and Des were out together in the early hours of the morning, they discovered an old homeless man lying on the street in a critical condition. They decided to bring him back to The Ark, and retrieved a broken wheelchair from the shelter. As they shunted him unsteadily away, they covered their faces with their T-shirts. The sweet and sickly smell of the man, caused by his consumption of *'gaveen',* a local alcoholics' cocktail of fluids that should rightly be used in car maintenance and which was rotting away his internal organs, was almost suffocating.

As they approached the Point Road, Dave noticed a solitary man walking ahead of them in a tatty leather jacket. From a side street two further men walked out, and began to gain quickly on him from the rear. Dave sensed that something was going to happen. He watched as one of the men drew a large bush knife, jogged in close behind, and brought it up under the man's ribs. The man slumped into the wall, and rolled over onto the pavement. Dave felt a cold sweat come over him. The muggers were only yards ahead of them.

He turned and looked at Des. "Just pray, keep walking, and everything will be okay for us," Des answered quietly.

As they passed by the huddle, the men were removing the man's jacket . The muggers looked uneasily across at them. They knew that their assault had been witnessed. Dave felt anger welling up inside him: the crime was ruthless and the spoils pathetic. He wanted to take the homeless man's crutch and hurl it at them. He looked at Des and then straight ahead, and they pushed the wheelchair on. They kept walking and didn't look back. As Dave looked down at the old man's lolling head, he thought about Des' self-assurance of their safety: it was a confidence of deep faith. Maybe they had just been lucky; somehow he sensed that this wasn't the case, and that they had been protected from a near certain assault.

As Dave continued to spend many of his days and evenings with Des, he learnt a great deal more about him. Des told him how he had been a member of the African National Congress through the troubled years of the Apartheid system, and how he had spent time in prison for assaulting a white police officer before turning to Christ himself. "I hated the whites," he confessed looking down at the stump of his finger.

Dave told Des about his 'firm' and the fighting at football matches and how he had been racist in his thinking. "I went to a National Front meeting once," he admitted. They laughed as they looked each other over again. Dave shook his head. It struck him as an incredible thing: here he was now, a Bristol 'casual' dependent on an Indian for his safety in a predominantly black neighbourhood of Durban.

Amongst the residents of The Ark, most of who had no resources of their own, it seemed to Dave that there was a necessary dependence on God into which He was graciously providing. It also seemed that God was moving in amazing ways amongst those who willingly opened their lives to Him, including his own. With a certain trepidation, he took a few further chances. Whilst he was buying a pair of summer shorts in a downtown Durban store, a black lady approached him. She told him that her daughter was seriously ill and had been taken into hospital. Dave looked around him, and then back at the clothing rack. Did she think that she knew him from somewhere? What had it got to do with him? Then he checked himself. Maybe God was telling him something here! He lay down the shorts and prayed with her in the middle of the shop floor.

The woman seemed visibly relieved and thanked him as she left. Dave felt moved by the incident. On another occasion, he felt a strong prompting to take a particular peroxide-haired teenager living at The Ark into the centre of the city. He was a little uncertain about it, but he figured that maybe God wanted him to get her a few treats: she was attending school wearing only donated clothes, and he had plenty of spare cash for his visit. After buying her a new pair of jeans and some make-up, they stopped in the shopping centre for a coffee and a doughnut.

As Dave sat sipping his drink, he sensed God prompting him to talk to the girl specifically about the opposite sex. 'Why me... of all people Lord?' he prayed inside. He took a few gulps of his drink.

"Erm... Natalie," he began tentatively, "you know you have to be careful with men... about their motives, don't you?"

He had barely finished his sentence when she began to sob like a child. Dave ran his hand down his face. He felt that he had really put his foot in it. "What's the matter?" he asked.

"Well... I think that I'm pregnant," the girl spluttered. He asked her a few more questions. From the way she described her symptoms, it seemed to him that she might actually have a sexually transmitted disease.

"Don't worry," he said trying to be reassuring, "we'll sort it out. We'll go see the doctor."

Dave looked around him. He couldn't believe how he'd got himself into this situation. He didn't have a clue where to take the girl. He didn't know anything about the medical facilities in the city. As they left the shopping centre together, he said a further prayer. 'Right Lord, you're going to have to help me out here.' 'Go into that tower block over there,' came the quiet answer somewhere in his thoughts.

Ahead of them was a modern office block. In the entrance foyer, Dave glanced over the company nameplates and spotted a medical insurance agency on the sixteenth floor. He figured that they might point him in the right direction.

Together, he and Natalie stepped into the lift. Outside the office, Dave looked at his reflection in the glass door. He was wearing a pair of old shorts, and was shirtless with his English rose and British Lion tattoos on full display. 'Oh God,' he thought. He knocked and entered, and asked the man sitting behind his desk if he could help them with a query.

"You're English, aren't you?" said the man in a thick scouse accent. Dave laughed to himself. "Well, I'm a missionary, and I need a little advice," he said. The man looked Dave up and down. "Oh yes," he said smirking, "and what church is that with?" Dave grinned back. He chatted with the man for a while and explained how he had come to work along the Point Road and about the situation with Natalie.

"Well, it just so happens that a friend of mine is one of the leading gynaecologists in Natal," the man replied. "I'll give him a call for you now." When the telephone conversation was over, an appointment had been arranged for later in the afternoon. Dave looked out of the office window and up at the clear, blue sky. He was gobsmacked. Later in the afternoon, at a private hospital with palm trees, fountains and a marble foyer, Natalie was given free medication for, as Dave had rightly suspected, a sexually transmitted disease.

Though Dave moaned about the food, and was never entirely comfortable with the living conditions during his two-month stay at The Ark, he knew that these things were an important part of the experience. He had leant on God much more in Durban when his comforts had been stripped away, than he'd ever done in Bristol. He made many friends at the centre, especially amongst some of the women residents, who gratefully received his little gifts of soap and toiletries. They were a treasured luxury for them.

The Ark football team were also indebted to him too after he haggled a deal with a local trader for an entire new green and white strip—at some cost to his own terrace-Protestant pride. His friendship with Des became a mainstay of the visit, despite the staining of one of his *Giorgio Armani* shirts when he accompanied him to the home of his Indian relatives to eat his first ever curry entirely with his fingers.

There were further experiences at The Ark that made a deep impression on him too. Early one humid evening, as he helped the centre's plump Afrikaner nurse in the sick bay, a disabled black man was brought in off the street and he needed to be deloused. Dave helped the nurse take off his trousers, and then lower him into the water of a rough concrete bath. The man looked up awkwardly at him. His eyes were bloodshot and wet. He was filthy and had soiled himself. He then looked down, away from Dave's gaze. Dave took a clean cloth from a nearby cupboard, and gently wiped the man's legs. He did not know what to say. "I'm… sorry," he stuttered.

He had never done such a thing for anyone. As he rinsed the cloth in the bath water, he felt as if something inside him was breaking. Shortly, he helped the man to sit upright, and then dabbed at the glistening beads of water on his back with a towel. He felt that he wanted to do this and more for him. He seemed so vulnerable. He knew this was an important moment in his life. He knew, if he could find a way to do it, that such work was what he wanted to do.

Chapter Nine

YEAR OF GRACE

Dave had not been back in Bristol for long when a friend casually made a suggestion that he had never seriously considered before his journey to South Africa. Every year at Henleaze and Westbury Church, a number of people joined a core team in the community known as the 'Year Team'. The group gave their time to the service of the other members of the congregation doing all manner of necessary duties.

"Why don't you join it Dave?" the friend suggested.

Dave thought about it over the next couple of days. Maybe it could be a good way to follow on from the desire that had grown inside him whilst he helped out at The Ark's sickbay and walked the Durban streets! He hesitated. It seemed to him, though, that they would probably just want educated and together people for the team, and he felt unsure if he qualified on either of those counts.

When he asked his pastor about it, his reply was unexpected. "I don't see why not," replied Dave Mitchell warmly. "I think it would be an excellent thing for you to do."

Dave was delighted. He felt a growing inkling of a new direction in his life. Back at his Clifton flat, he punched the air with excitement.

The first thing he needed to do after he was formally accepted on the team was to raise himself enough financial support. The position was a full-time one for those who undertook it; so it was not possible to claim any state benefits, and difficult to do paid employment at the same time.

Dave sat alone on the settee in his living room, and took his financial needs to God in prayer. As had happened when he was struggling to meet his bills and wondering about his trip to South Africa, the money was provided. Before long, with a little help from his mother, five pound-coins that arrived every week in a brown envelope from an unknown donor, and other small regular gifts, his basic needs were met with a small amount for luxuries on top.

Woodlands fellowship had recently rented a large Victorian property, near the city's University, owned by The George Muller Foundation. Its rooms were vast and spacious; even if their decoration had been a little neglected over the years. A live-in community of 'Year Team' members, including Dave Mitchell and his family, however, began to fill up the place with a buzz of human activity. A large room on the top floor with a sloping roof was made available for Dave, and he packed up the remainder of his belongings from his flat, and moved them across to his new home.

As Dave settled down to living in community, it was a challenge for him and others to make it work. He had never had to live with people in such a way before, sharing the house's kitchen, washing facilities, food and other amenities. In the past, if things weren't to his liking, he had kicked up a fuss to get what he wanted.

At the community house he learnt much about having to get along with other people, and giving way to their needs. It was a time filled with some rough lessons for himself, and those who were living with him. If Dave felt that anyone was having a go at him, or anyone he cared about, he was still prone to flying off the handle.

One time, when a team member repeatedly wound him up about a matter, Dave couldn't restrain himself any longer. He charged after the man into the kitchen and pursued him around the large wooden dining table. His mind had blanked out all other thoughts but giving him the 'slap' he deserved.

Fortunately, he evaded Dave's wrath by dancing anxiously around the piece of furniture until Dave had cooled off a little. Other members of the team watched on in polite astonishment. They had never had to deal with anyone like Dave before.

Eventually, though, he learnt a little more self-control, and some of his rougher edges received a gentle filing down. His direct, no-nonsense manner in team meetings, however, did shake a few people out of their complacency. He told others flatly when he thought they were spending too much on PA systems and not enough on the poor. If Dave sensed an injustice, he would let it be known, even if he sometimes made mistakes.

When a gang of outside builders were paid for doing work on the church and he wasn't, he told the community leaders what he thought of them. "You're just like everyone else, out for what you can get, and you're fleecing me in the process," he shouted. When it was quietly pointed out that such things were actually a part of his 'Year Team' duties, he saw the error of his judgement and apologised. He felt like a hotheaded fool.

In truth, he'd had a further reason for protesting. He'd wanted the money for a particular self-indulgence that he still held dearly on to. On his new reduced level of income, he couldn't afford to buy the items of designer clothing he still craved. Recently, Dave had mooched around the fashion store windows in the city centre, and spotted a particular blue *Stone Island* jacket and some *Adidas* training shoes that he wanted.

Back in his room at the community house, he let God know what he thought of his fatherly care. "You said in your word that you would provide for those who follow you," he moaned. "Here I am without the cash for a pair of shoes!"

The following day, as if in answer to his prayer, he was given a gift of money sufficient to cover the cost of the items. Later, when he had tossed the carrier bags and wrapping paper to one side, and laid the items on his bed with a ceremonial care, a sinking feeling came over him. He knew that he didn't really need them; he felt like a spoilt teenager. They remained uncomfortably in his wardrobe from then on, a lesson, he felt, in his own vanity.

Dave's 'Year Team' duties involved doing the many and various tasks needed to ensure the smooth running of the life of the fellowship and its buildings. He would set out the chairs and clear up after meetings, keep an eye on security during the services, and sometimes do building maintenance work.

A particularly humbling task for Dave was helping to prepare and serve the free lunches the church laid on for students at the nearby University. His general dislike of them was a lingering prejudice that he had to face up to, and spending this time with them helped him in some measure to deal with it. The task that he relished above all others, however, was encouraging and praying with both those in the congregation who needed a little support, and others who came in from the outside community.

One time, a gaunt, pale-skinned man wandered into the church asking for some food to eat. Dave talked with him, and the next day walked the short distance to his flat to visit. There, he discovered the conditions in which the man and an alcoholic relative were living: a couple of derelict rooms with glass, filth and syringes scattered across the floorboards. Dave kept in contact with them, and when they were eventually rehoused by the council, he hired a van and drove their possessions to their new home.

On another occasion, as he left a church meeting, he came across a homeless woman sitting bent up on the steps. He sat briefly and prayed with her, and then encouraged her to find shelter for the night. Around midnight, the thought of her still out in the cold unsettled him, and he returned with some coffee and chocolate, and then stayed with her for a while. Not long after, she began to attend the church.

Dave regularly spent time with other homeless individuals who squatted in blankets outside the nearby shops asking for spare change. Sometimes he would talk and pray with them or take out food parcels; other times he would invite them along to church, or point them in the right direction for different social services.

He also began to make visits into the nearby Horfield Prison to help with the running of basic Christianity courses, and into hospitals to pray at bedsides if someone requested a visitor from the church. He discovered that there were many who were comfortable talking to him because of his background: they knew that he, like themselves, was no whiter than white character. He in turn found an increasing pleasure and purpose in drawing alongside people to give them his attention and support.

In addition to praying for individuals, Dave accompanied a team from his fellowship on a series of visits to pray around the floors of a newly built office block close to Bristol's docks. The building's managers were troubled by a range of strange phenomena on their premises, which had been built on a site used in the eighteenth century for the transportation of African slaves. The cleaners were complaining of cold atmospheres and refusing to work, and the lift kept stalling at a certain floor and its German engineers were unable to find any fault with it. They were having real difficulties letting the office space as a consequence. The managers had tried various other ways of tackling the situation with little result, and thought they would now give Christianity a try.

As Dave and other members of the church walked through the building praying, they came across a number of rooms in which there was an overwhelming smell of sweat and vomit, and an unusual coldness in the air. Dave's head was spinning with the strength of it, and he had to steady himself on the wall. When he was prayed for, however, the sensation eased. After returning on a number of occasions to pray through the building, and also with some of its staff, the phenomena disappeared, the lift began to work properly, and many of the employees were set at peace about the situation. Dave felt privileged that God had used him in such a way in the heart of the city's business community.

A full day of Bible teaching sessions was a further key part of the program for 'Year Team' members. Every Wednesday, they would gather together for a range of seminars and lectures held at The George Muller Foundation. On these days, Dave wanted to learn, yet, as had always been the case at school, he struggled to do it in such a context. He just couldn't seem to take things in, and he would scribble restlessly on his paper and glance around. When others made time to teach him on a one to one basis, though, his knowledge came on in leaps and bounds. Around this time, Dave was also assigned a personal mentor who he could talk and pray through personal issues with, and this made him feel that someone else was looking out for him when he needed it.

At pubs in the city centre and along the busy Gloucester Road, Dave continued to meet up on a weekend with his mates. A Saturday night out on the town, with its fights and pints and the hunt for girls to pick up, had been such a loved institution in his life that he wanted to see if he could remain in the old scene in a way that reflected his Christian faith.

He also craved the warmth of the lads' friendship. The fighting itself no longer held any attraction for him. If he sensed that a situation might develop, he would steer well clear of it. The prospect of violence made him sick. He would also try to keep his intake of alcohol down to a reasonable level, but sometimes after the first pint or two, the following ones seemed to drink themselves.

In the past, Dave's treatment of women too had left a lot to be desired. On a Sunday morning, faced with someone he had picked up on the dancefloor looking at him from the adjacent pillow, he'd wanted to get rid of her, and had curtly tossed her a ten pound note for a taxi cab home, irrespective of the emotional consequences for both the girl or himself. Now, even though he set out with a new conscience and the best of intentions, and even try to evangelise girls that he met, he would still fall prey to his own weakness. The trend, however, eventually turned in the right direction.

On an occasion at a party on the outskirts of the city, Dave had had a couple of drinks and could feel himself edging close to wooziness. One girl, who had been coming on strong for much of the evening, began to make a number of graphic invitations. Dave's mind flashed agonisingly between the prospect and his sense of the right way to play the situation. This time, he made a quick excuse that he needed to find the toilet, and slipped quietly out of the back door. Once outside in the night air, he jogged down from the party under the warm, orange streetlighting to the city centre, smiling and praising God that he had had the strength to live up to his own principles.

Later, a friend who had seen him running along with a wide grin on his face quizzed him about it. "What was happening with you last night?" he asked curiously.

Dave didn't think it worth a full explanation. "Oh, I was just having a good time," he smiled.

On earlier occasions, though, by the uneasy expression on Dave's face in the Sunday services, it was apparent to others that his Saturday nights out had left him feeling guilty and dissatisfied with himself. Often, he would ask someone to sit in a corner of the church with him and listen to his prayers of confession. One decisive time, as he waited in the presence of the Holy Spirit, Dave saw a vivid mental picture of two planets floating side by side in the midst of dark space. One of the planets glowed blue like the Earth illuminated in the sun's rays: the other was in darkness. In the scene, Dave was jumping backwards and forwards freely between the two worlds.

He understood the meaning of the picture: he was trying to hop between his old ways and his new life in Christ, and he knew which he had to choose. Some of his old friends had already decided that his new behaviour was not to their liking, and they had drawn away from him.

But over the next couple of months, as he consciously pulled further away from his old scene, he felt a terrible bleakness and loneliness. As he sat on the crumpled blankets of his bed at the community house Wendy, a caring girl with dark shoulder-length hair who was also on the 'Year Team', knocked softly and peered around his bedroom door. She walked across the bare wooden floor, sat alongside him and smiled with concern. He knew that she understood what he was feeling. He was deeply glad for her and the people in his fellowship. Right now he felt carried by their commitment to him. Though some of his old attachments were fraying and breaking, he had never known relationships like these before in his life, and he thanked God silently inside for them.

Much of the inner turbulence that had once clouded around Dave's heart and mind lifted away as a consequence of persistent prayer at the church. He let go of the scores that he had once wanted to settle. In the past, when he had come across anyone who he felt had hurt him or put him down, he had wanted to pay them back with interest. There were pupils and teachers at Lawrence Weston School especially who Dave would have dearly relished returning a fist full of humiliation to, and one or two pupils who crossed his path again in later life and got one. On the night the two students prayed for him at Bristol Community Church, he knew that God had forgiven him for the acts that he had committed against others and himself.

From then on, he in turn felt able to forgive and be released from a semi-conscious hit list of revenge that was knotting him up inside. For the people that Dave had hurt himself in fights at football matches and in pubs, he knew that in many cases there was little he could do by way of individual recompense, except remain open to the future possibilities of circumstance. He had also damaged himself emotionally in the midst of his own violence, and he still carried the wounds, though some had now been tended to by God's healing touch. But for certain people he had crossed, he said his own `private prayers, asking for forgiveness again, and that in some way at a future point in time they might be generously blessed by God's favour as a measure of compensation.

Since Dave had begun attending Henleaze and Westbury church, he had stood up in public regularly to talk about his past and some of the good things that God had done for him. He had done this at other churches and youth groups, at a summer camp organised by the London church Holy Trinity Brompton, and for the Christian Football League. On these occasions, a number of people approached him to say that they too had been involved in similar things, and felt that few people in their fellowships understood their experiences and feelings. Dave was able to assure them that he did, and he prayed with more than one for the strength to keep walking on with God under the weight of their own histories.

A special public opportunity, however, arose for Dave at this time when he was invited to record his story for a video broadcast to be shown at the 'There's More To Life' mission to Bristol, led by the Argentinean evangelist Luis Palau. Dave was accompanied by a film crew into the stand of Bristol City's football ground, Ashton Gate, to produce a short piece that was eventually broadcast there before the gathered thousands.

As he sat facing the camera, he looked down at the green pitch mown neatly in lines below him, and at the rows of empty red seats around the stands, and he reflected back. It seemed an incredible circumstance that he should be recording such a thing at all, let alone at the 'City' ground, on the terrace where he had once hurled abuse at Rovers' arch-enemies the 'Robins', yet it seemed the most appropriate of venues.

Dave continued to attend matches at the Rovers ground throughout his time on the 'Year team'. His love of football remained as strong as it had ever been, and his devotion to Rovers, 'The Pirates', was unchanged. He stuck to his taste in clothing, the distinctive choices of a 'casual', though he no longer wanted to take part in any of the rituals: the taunting, face-offs and fights with rival 'boys'. He also found himself dropping the cuss words from many of the chants and choruses as they rose around him in the crowds – most of the time at least.

When he didn't, his old mates would seize instantly on the opportunity for a dose of teasing. "Hark at him, lads!" "Language, Jesus!" Sometimes, members of Dave's church fellowship would join him on the terraces to watch home games, much to the amusement of some of the Rovers 'boys'.

"Is this your new 'firm' then Dave?" someone would rib him.

"Yes," Dave would reply with a seriousness and a grin. "It's God's 'firm'."

On more than one occasion, when away fans stole in amongst the Rovers supporters and trouble broke out, Dave's presence drew an old friend away from joining in the fighting. "I think I'll stand with you and the God squad this time," one lad said pensively, blowing into his hands to warm them up.

Chapter Ten

KING DAVID

When Dave first met Nikki, a blonde, self-assured obstetrician from a privileged background in Belfast, he had written her off as a posh doctor—though a not unattractive one. Her upbringing, he thought, was way too remote from his to make anything more of it. Nikki, however, telephoned Dave to invite him out for a drink, and soon they began to see each other as friends. Dave quickly sussed out that Nikki was interested; as a well practised flirting man he could spot all the signals without too much difficulty, and he felt rather pleased with himself. One afternoon, whilst Dave was still serving on the 'Year Team', Nikki called him and asked if he could help her with preparation for an examination she had shortly with the Royal College of Gynaecologists and Obstetricians.

"Well.. I suppose I could, if you like," said Dave, with one or two anxious reservations about what practical use he might be.

In his room at the community house, Dave sat facing Nikki on a small soft chair. She was waiting for him to start the exercise. He glanced nervously over the multi-choice examination paper that she wanted him to read out, question by question, so she could practice giving her answers. The paper was riddled with terminology troublesome enough for a qualified doctor to pronounce. Dave, however, felt determined not to let her see that he had any difficulty reading. He did not want her thinking that he was stupid.

He began: "The recognised complications of a Wer...theim's hyster... hysterectomy include. A) retro... peritonial... hae.. matoma." He soldiered on determinedly, the sweat forming in cold beads across his forehead. "B) lymph... lymph... oedema."

After twenty minutes, Dave felt desperate for a break and some fresh air, and he invited her up to the roof of the house. The view from the top spread down over the suburban chimney pots and skylights past the University tower and towards the centre of Bristol. As he looked at Nikki, he wondered what impression he had made as he'd read from the exam paper. He liked her, even if she seemed too educated. She walked a couple of paces closer to him. He sensed something in her glance; he knew what was about to happen. He leant towards her, brushing her cheek softly with tip of his nose, and they kissed for the first time.

Dave continued to see Nikki over the next couple of months, calling around at her nearby flat. He reflected with amusement on their differences: she liked strawberries and he liked bananas, she Champagne and he lager, but he nevertheless felt a special something for her. Dave began to spend time with her son Rob, and took him along to Rovers matches.

As he made his way past the parked cars along Nikki's avenue one time, he sensed God letting him know that it was time to stop messing about in relationships. He needed to make a decision one way or another, and not string this situation along.

Shortly, he decided to put it to her. "If you want to get married, you've got to do the asking," he said with a grin on his face.

On a blustery Christmas Eve, 1997, Dave married Nikki at the fellowship's new meeting place, Woodlands Christian Centre, on a leafy avenue close to the University. It was a relaxed and happy day for them both. Dave Mitchell was the presiding minister, and as he dropped the rings they rolled inconveniently into the congregation. Dave got Nikki's name wrong during the ceremony, and they both collapsed into laughter. During the signing of the register, Dave had set up a video screen to play the England goals from the 1966 World Cup Final against West Germany—to give the ceremony a lighter touch. He could hear his mates cheering along as he and family members penned their names in the register in a small side chapel.

As Dave sang 'Be Thou My Vision', his choice for a service hymn, he felt humbled and deeply thankful to God. It reminded him that his commitment to Nikki was a part of how much he had changed as a person. That evening, when he moved into Nikki's flat, he felt a sadness about leaving the friends he had grown close to at the community house. But he felt that he had found the right woman, and a deeper sense of contentment began to settle over him.

A little over a month after the wedding ceremony, with both Nikki and Dave Mitchell's help, Dave made a crucial and long-overdue discovery. Incidents on the 'Year Team' were highlighting an ever present issue. Whenever Dave had been asked to fill out Bible study course forms, he would blankly refuse. Sometimes he would even rip them up in a defiant panic. Secretly, he didn't want the risk of anyone looking over his shoulder at what he wrote in case he jumbled up his letters. He felt deeply sensitive about the matter. It was a feeling that went back to his school days: of not wanting anyone to chastise him for poor written work. As long as Dave could remember, he'd had difficulty with words, as well as with concentrating and retaining information, and remembering sequences of instructions – after the third or fourth one, they would all become mixed up in his head.

One afternoon, as Dave struggled to write down a telephone number in Dave Mitchell's office, his pastor made a suggestion. "Dave, you know, I think that you might be dyslexic. Why don't you go get a test?"

Dave was a little unsure what it meant, let alone having considered that he might suffer from such a thing before. That evening in the kitchen, he talked it over with Nikki, who encouraged him to make an appointment with an Educational Psychologist. As a preparation for the coming evaluation, she passed him a book of IQ problem-solving activities to see how he got on. Dave sat flicking through the pages at the kitchen table, and then hurled the book away from him. He felt so frustrated with himself: he just wanted to be able to do them and he couldn't.

When the day of the test came, he paced around outside the front of the psychologist's house drawing heavily on a cigarette. He knew that the outcome would let him know whether he really was 'con-Jeal' the 'clot' that he'd been labelled at school, or if some form of disability had always hampered him.

At a large mahogany table in the doctor's dining room, she gave him a full two-hour intelligence test. The results were a confirmation of Dave Mitchell's suspicions. Dave was shown to be suffering from 'clear and significant' dyslexia, and far from lacking in intelligence, in the majority of sub-tests he scored well above average. Furthermore, his perceptual organisation was within the top 5% of the population. Despite seeing educational psychologists during his years at school, his dyslexia had never been diagnosed. Dave now knew that throughout all that time, his classroom performance hadn't been poor as a result of him being merely lazy or stupid. He felt a tremendous sense of relief, and deeply vindicated by the test results. It was like a gift from God.

In the summer of 1998, it was the turn of France to play host nation to football's biggest and best international tournament, the World Cup. On Dave's instigation, the large video screen was erected in church for all the England games, and the building filled up with enthusiastic England fans from both within the congregation and outside. When England scored, the chairs went tumbling over in the exuberant atmosphere, and the events were a big community-building success. Dave obtained tickets for England's game against Tunisia in Marseilles, and he, Rob and Nikki, now heavily pregnant with their child, drove down the French motorway system to the Mediterranean coast.

All through the journey, Dave listened to the radio reports of trouble between the gathering England supporters and the thousands of Tunisians and other North Africans in the city. He felt a growing sense of unease about attending the game in the midst of such an environment, for his family's safety, and because the scene was all too familiar. On the day before the match, when they drove the car along the sea front past the groups of England supporters singing outside the bars, he could feel the bad atmosphere in the city and it reminded him of Stockholm.

That evening, they stayed in the nearby town of Aix-en-Provence, and the following morning Nikki dropped Dave and Rob off in the city centre before driving back up country for a day's sightseeing. As Dave and Rob walked around the shops and cafes near the harbour, groups of English and Tunisian fans were taunting each other and scuffles were breaking out. Ahead of them, one Tunisian with a red and white scarf tied around his forehead like a martial arts fighter hurled a wooden stick across the street at some English men. They whistled and jeered back at him. Dave was feeling increasingly nervous and edgy, and he steered Rob away along a quieter street.

Closer to the stadium the situation worsened. As the thousands of rival supporters mingled together, scuffles escalated into running battles. A hail of glass and debris was being tossed backwards and forwards across the approach road as groups charged kicking and punching each other. Dave hoisted Rob under his arm and ran away with crowds of others as the violence spread out around him, and bottles came shattering down on the pavement surface. When he heard the chants of 'We are England... We are England...' he felt the adrenaline and an old sense of bullish national pride well up inside him.

'Yes,' he thought, 'I am England, and this is a right liberty. Who on earth do these Tunisians think they are?' He thought about joining in with the England fans so he could give the Tunisians a proper kicking for threatening him and endangering his stepson. He was breathing heavily. He looked around him; there were some England lads beckoning to a crowd of Arabs ahead on the road. He felt pulled in two directions. His old self wanted to run away with him. He held his mind in check for a moment, and then took himself to one side, closed his eyes, and prayed under his breath. He began to feel calmer, and he knew he did not want any part of it. When he opened his eyes, Rob was looking at him enquiringly. Dave smiled back through the tension in his face, and they made their way around the crowds and the riot police towards the stadium entrance.

That evening, back in Aix-en-Provence, Dave was feeling a little higher in his spirits due to England's 2-0 victory over the North Africans. When he, Nikki and Rob left the hotel in search of a restaurant, however, they walked into a further situation. As they made their way past the busy bars and shops along the town's main street, a group of Tunisian youths walked past them wearing red and white scarves. The young men looked them coldly up and down. A few seconds later, Dave felt a stone strike him on the back of his head. He spun around to face them. The

Tunisians bounced back cockily towards them.

Dave's first thought was for Nikki and Rob. He dreaded that something might happen to them. The situation was like a sudden old nightmare. The youths crowded swiftly around them and began to face up to Dave beckoning to him to start something. Dave felt the muscles in his arms and neck draw tighter. He did not want to get into a fight with these boys, but he felt that if any of them touched his pregnant wife or Rob, he would struggle to restrain himself. He scanned the eyes of all the youths, ready to spot the first one who made a move. He was sweating and shaking.

The stand off continued as the long seconds passed. Dave felt torn through again between how he would once have dealt with them, giving them the 'slap' they deserved, and a strong will within him to avoid violence and turn the other cheek. He prayed that God would send someone to their assistance, though he half wished it would be a crowd of furious England supporters to give them a right 'shoeing'. 'Oh, Lord. Please help us,' he cried out inside. He continued to watch the eyes of each member of the gang. A passing family walked over and spoke some words to the youths in French. They seemed to back off a little and then try to laugh the incident off. Dave was reeling inside, but he heaved a sigh of relief. They were all safe, and he had managed not to cross the line for a second time.

It was little more than a couple of months after they returned from Marseilles that Nikki gave birth to a baby girl weighing five pounds and twelve ounces. Dave was watching football on the television with his mates when the moment of arrival shook him from his entertainment, and he rushed his wife into the hospital where she worked as an obstetrician. Dave felt in a helpless panic about the event: Nikki, however, was reassuringly familiar with the process. The following day, after a difficult delivery in which the umbilical cord became caught around the baby's neck, Hannah was born two weeks prematurely but in good health.

Dave had somehow known for over two weeks which date would be the one, October 22nd. In the family-friendly delivery theatre the midwife handed him his tiny, wet daughter, and he placed her inside his *Burberry* shirt against the warmth of his skin. She was so beautiful and vulnerable and dependent now on his care. Dave could feel the tears welling up in his eyes. He was so pleased with himself and with Nikki.

A little while later, he took out a small bottle of scented oil that he had prepared specially, and let a few drops fall onto his daughter's forehead. The fragrance was sweet in the air. He wanted to dedicate her to God, to hand her over to His care, yet still keep a hold of her. He prayed quietly under his breath, thanking God for her and asking Him to take care of her throughout her life. He sensed that he was glimpsing God's fatherly love in a new way. He knew that he wanted to give good things to Hannah without expecting to receive anything back, and that whatever she did in her life he would love and forgive her.

A special position was created for Dave that autumn as the Social Action Officer for Woodlands fellowship, after he had served on the church's 'year team' for two years. He had wanted to continue with the work he'd been doing, and it was recognised by the leadership that he had a particular gift for drawing alongside a range of people in their needs. Dave could do it in a way that was natural to him, and was felt to be genuine by those he spent time with.

His past had left him familiar with many things. He knew what it was to feel hurt and downtrodden, and what the trigger points for violence were. He knew how it felt to behave in an outrageous manner, to be held in the grip of fear and evil, and to be desperately needy. He was perhaps less inclined to judge others for their behaviour as a consequence.

Dave became involved in a range of projects and initiatives with Woodlands fellowship. He managed a new community house for members of the church who needed the company of others to help them grow and thrive in their faith—like he had once needed. He helped in the running of a special home set up as a first step out of detoxification for alcohol and drug abusers. He became a source of personal support for those within the fellowship struggling with sexual and other life-controlling issues, making referrals, supplying information and lending a listening ear. He also visited and gave support to many within the wider community including homeless people and those struggling with substance addictions, and he set up a daytime access church within the fellowship specifically for them.

The one thing he enjoyed in his work more than anything, though, was talking to others about the love of God, and the real possibilities for change that it brought. A couple of visiting speakers at the church spoke out a public prophecy during a service for Dave. In the future, they felt that he would in a way be like Israel's King David, as recorded in the Old Testament's books of Samuel. He too would have his own flock of disgruntled and marginalized people looking to him for advice and counsel. When he heard the words, he felt like God was slipping a royal ring onto his finger. He hoped that this might truly be the way in which he could serve Him in his life; it was a challenge he felt increasingly ready and equipped for.

Some time before his appointment as Woodlands Social Action Officer, Dave travelled back to South Africa to visit Des, and to meet up with many of the old acquaintances he had made during his stay at The Ark. One evening whilst staying along the Point Road, he accompanied Des and a hardy Afrikaner woman, Renée, once more onto the Durban Streets with the centre's nightly outreach team.

As they walked past a seafront bar, they came across the scene of an assault. Three hefty Afrikaner men had surrounded a black African, and were repeatedly punching the man as he lay sprawled on the pavement at their feet. The men yelled abuse at him drunkenly, and then ran forward kicking him viciously in the back and ribs. The African moaned and pleaded for them to stop. For a few moments, Dave watched the man bouncing around like a cloth doll, his head red with blood. Then he felt incensed by what he was seeing; he could not bear to watch it.

Without looking at Des or Renée, he shouted at the men, "Oi... What do you think you are doing? Leave him!" He ran towards them. They looked up hesitantly. He slowed his pace down to a walk and strode into the centre of the group. The men stood panting and looking uneasily at each other and at Dave.

One man cursed him. Another took a step towards him. Dave now realised his risk; never as a 'casual' would he have taken it. He looked at the men levelly as he drew in deep lung-fulls of air. Renée arrived and began to speak to the men in Afrikaans. They seemed uncomfortable in her presence. After a couple of minutes, they turned and left, straightening their clothes.

Dave helped the man to his feet. "We'll get you cleaned up," he said.

The group then walked across the seafront road to a rickety shower pipe on the nearby beach. As the man stood unsteadily, Dave turned the water handle and took out a handkerchief from his pocket. He wiped the man's face and forehead and rinsed out the blood under the spray. The man looked at Dave, his eyes straining to focus.

Dave glanced back at Renée and Des. Passers by were gathering around the scene and watching curiously. Dave felt a lump swelling in his throat and the backs of his eyes began to prick with tears. He felt ashamed. He wanted to apologise—for the sins of his fellow whites, and for many other things. "I'm sorry," he said. "I'm sorry for the things that have been done to you."

The man looked back and nodded. The threesome gathered around and prayed for the man, and then, when he seemed a little better, they walked away steadily along the sand.

BRISTOL ROVERS FOOTBALL CLUB P.L.C.

FOUNDED 1883

Reg. No. 51828 England
VAT Reg. No. 137 4967 35

Registered Office:
468 Stapleton Road,
Eastville,
Bristol, BS5 6PA.
Telephones: (S.T.D. code 0272)
Office and Commercial: 510363 and 510828
Manager: 573837

Stadium:
Twerton Park, Bath.
Telephone: (0225) 312327

Please address all correspondence
to the Registered Office.

10 October 1986

RECORDED DELIVERY

D Jeal Esq.,
Bristol

Dear David Jeal,

Misconduct at Bristol Rovers v Black pool Match and at Bristol Rovers v Chesterfield Match

I am advised by the Police that at both the above matches on 27th September and 3rd October they found it necessary to eject you for abusive behaviour.

I am writing therefore to inform you that the Club has decided to exercise their rights under paragraph 15 of the Ground Regulations to bar you entry to Twerton Park for Bristol Rovers home football matches until after 31st July 1991.

If you enter, or attempt to enter the Twerton Park premises during the currency of this bar, you will be liable for prosecution by the Club in the County Court for damages for trespass.

The Club has made it clear publicly on many occasions that they will not tolerate misconduct of any kind.

(Yours sincerely, etc ...)

Transcript of a letter received by Dave

Last thought

Feel free to email me if anything you have read in this book leaves you with questions. If you want God to help you to sort your life out then pray this prayer. He always hears and always answers but sometimes not in the way we expect! *God knows the score!*

> Dear God,
> I know that I mess things up on my own. I just ask you now to help me to turn away from my old life. I thank you that Jesus died on the cross so that I can be forgiven for all the bad stuff I have ever done. I just ask you now to fill me with your Holy Spirit and to give me the strength to follow you, Lord. *Amen*

If you have prayed this prayer then talk about it with someone who is a Christian. Or you can email me and I will try and sort you out with a Church and someone to talk stuff through with.

God Bless You

Dave Jeal
    email: davejeal@blueyonder.co.uk

More on Dave Jeal

Readers may be interested to know how God has carried on blessing Dave Jeal's life. Having heard the call of ministry Dave started chaplaincy work in 1999 at HMP Ashfield - a juvenile prison holding some four hundred young men at any one time. He loved this job so much that he remains there to this day!

In June 2005, he and his wife Nikki started up a new church with local people in the disused St James' Church, on the estate of Lockleaze in Bristol. The church continues to grow.

Dave's story has taken a further, somewhat ironic twist. In July 2007, he was asked to be chaplain to Bristol Rovers, the very club from which he was barred way back in 1986. Dave considers this calling to be a huge privilege: "I look forward to serving God, whatever he asks me to do and wherever he places me. I thank Jesus for all he has done, for me and through me."